ARMIES OF GOD

Strategies of Victory for Spiritual Warfare

by
DALE M. YOCUM

AUTHOR OF

Conformed to Christ
Creeds in Contrast
Dr Yocum Teaches the Epistles of Paul
Fruit Unto Holiness
God, The Master Scientist
Hijacker in the House
The Holy Way
Job, The Perfect Man
The People's Favorites
The Security of Holiness
Study Notes From My Bible
This Present World
With Peter by the Sea

SCHMUL PUBLISHING COMPANY
NICHOLASVILLE, KENTUCKY

Published by Schmul Publishing Co.
PO Box 776
Nicholasville, KY 40340

Printed in the United States of America

ISBN 10: 0-88019-223-2
ISBN 13: 978-0-88019-223-1

Visit us on the Internet at www.wesleyanbooks.com, or order direct from the publisher by calling 800-772-6657, or by writing to the above address.

CONTENTS

CHAPTER   PAGE

   Introduction   5
1 War In Heaven   7
2 The Holy War   11
3 Israel, God's Army   23
4 The Church, God's Army   35
5 Victory at Damascus   47
6 When God Goes to War   58
7 Conflict with Three Kings   63
8 God's Gift of Jericho   68
9 Learning From Failure   76
10 Star Wars   81
11 Strategy for Success   90
12 Is There Not a Cause?   94
13 Battle Plan for Victory   104
14 Strength for the Battle   108
15 Good Soldiers of Jesus Christ   116
16 Home-Trained Soldiers   125
17 War With the Lamb   133

INTRODUCTION

The inspiration for the theme of this book came to me quite by accident. I had written a series of editorials for a missionary magazine in which I was elucidating some principles for the missionary operation of the Church. It was quite surprising to discover that without prior intent I had drawn several of these from stories of Old Testament battles. Perhaps I had found a major theme that runs through the Word. Some research into the stories of Bible battles demonstrated that indeed I had—that the record of warfare in Israel contains many of the major principles that apply to the Church in her missionary battles.

A further portion of this material was first presented as a continuing series of short radio messages. Those portions have been transcribed and edited for publication, along with other chapters, in book form.

In making a study of this kind there are two possible courses of development. First, the more systematic way would be to collect the missionary principles of the Church and to seek support and illustration for them from the major conflicts in the Bible. The second would be to take the Bible records of battle chronologically and draw out whatever principles were found in them. The second approach has been chosen because it more closely parallels the development of the theme in my mind and allows a closer adherence to Biblical chronology.

Whatever apparent lack of organization is observed, the reader will please excuse because of the diversity in writing style: editorials, radio script and chapters for a book.

This series of studies is designed to help us who are members of God's church to be better soldiers in the battle. It will establish the fact that we *are* to be soldiers. Just as Israel was God's fighting army in Old Testament days, the Church is today. Our battles are not with physical weapons as theirs often were, but we are in a warfare just as real and just as demanding. By studying some of those Old Testament battles, we will find God's principles, *strategies of victory*, which apply to the church in our efforts to fulfil God's purposes for her in this age.

Special thanks are due to my daughters, Phyllis Marshall, for taking the various forms of the manuscript and adapting them to the final form; and Carmen Russell, for assisting in the editing of the manuscript.

My thanks also goes to my faithful wife, Ilene, who devotedly checked the script, made changes in the computer records, and printed the manuscript copies.

Finally, I am deeply indebted to Rev. Rex Bullock, director of DAYSPRING Radio, who encouraged the writing and arranged for the publication.

I hope YOU are in the battle on God's side. For certainly, my friend, you are on one side or the other: on God's side or Satan's side. And I want you to be on the winning side. God is going to win the battle and the OVERCOMERS will reign with Him forever! So come—it's enlisting time! Get into the fight for truth and gain the victory through Jesus Christ.

Dale M. Yocum
Shawnee, Kansas
March, 1987

EDITOR'S NOTE: Dr. Yocum went home to be with his Lord on Sunday, May 10, 1987. He lived to know that the manuscript was completed before his passing.

—Donna Cary

1

WAR IN HEAVEN

Did you know that virtually every battle fought on earth is just a temporal manifestation of a larger battle in the heavenlies—a warfare between God and Satan? There is much at stake in this warfare, and it includes the eternal destiny of every one of us.

To begin a study of this theme we will turn to the portion of John's prophecy found in Revelation 12:7-9.

> And there was war in heaven: Michael and his angels fought against the dragon; and the dragon fought and his angels and prevailed not; neither was their place found any more in heaven. And the great dragon was cast out, that old serpent, called the Devil, and Satan, which deceiveth the whole world: he was cast out into the earth, and his angels were cast out with him.

THE BATTLE

This is no minor skirmish—no mere war game. This is desperate warfare on a colossal scale. Just three verses earlier we are told that the dragon—the Devil—drew one-third of all the stars of heaven after him. They evidently represent fallen angels, for in II Peter 2:4 we read that ". . . God spared not the angels that sinned, but cast them down to hell, and delivered them into chains of darkness, to be reserved unto judgment."

These verses in Revelation 12 point both backward and forward. They point to that distant past when Satan sought to usurp the power of God and was cast out of heaven, apparently taking about one-third of all the angels of God with him. Jesus said, "I beheld Satan as lightning fall from heaven" (Luke 10:18). His first fall brought him to the lower heaven, the aerial region about the earth. St. Paul described Satan's hosts as "rulers of the darkness of this world," as wicked spirits in the heavenlies (Eph. 6:12). He also called Satan "the prince of the power of the air" (Eph. 2:2). Here in the atmospheric realm about the earth, demonic spirits move freely from place to place, seducing sinners, blinding the minds of unbelievers, and injecting suggestions and accusations into the minds of anybody who will receive them. They never sleep but work incessantly to generate doubts, false accusations, suspicions, delusions, false doctrines, temptations, discouragements and despair.

The verses under consideration point also to the future. There is coming a day, described in Revelation 12, when Satan's forces will be cast out of the heavenly region altogether—cast down to the earth, where with great wrath they will increase the measure of their fury, knowing their time is short.

Much of the book of Revelation is marked by the force of this battle. At times it seems Satan is winning, for in Revelation 13:7 it is written, "It was given [the antichrist] to make war with the saints, and to overcome them: and power was given him over all kindreds, and tongues, and nations." That victory over the saints is just on the physical level, of course, for the antichrist does not have power to force the human will into subjection to himself.

There is no doubt about the final outcome of this conflict, of course. While the chapters of Revelation resound with the shock of battle, the outcome is climactic and sure. Jesus will win, and His followers will reign with Him forever! There is no uncertainty about that; praise the Lord! We know Who will win. And we now have the opportunity to align ourselves on the winning side.

THE VICTORY

The climactic show-down is often called "The Battle of Armageddon." It's described for us in Revelation 19. We shall return to it later, but for now let's just look at a few verses describing the victory of Christ. "And I saw heaven opened, and behold a white horse; and he that sat upon him was called Faithful and

True, and in righteousness he doth judge and make war. . . . And the armies which were in heaven followed him upon white horses clothed in fine linen, white and clean. And out of his mouth goeth a sharp sword, that with it he should smite the nations: and he shall rule them with a rod of iron: and he treadeth the winepress of the fierceness and wrath of Almighty God. . . . And the beast was taken, and with him the false prophet that wrought miracles before him, with which he deceived them that had received the mark of the beast, and them that worshiped his image. These both were cast alive into a lake of fire burning with brimstone. . . . And he laid hold on the dragon, that old serpent, which is the Devil, and Satan, and bound him a thousand years." The crescendo of victory rises higher and higher right to the end of the Book. The followers of Jesus have rewards: thrones of authority, glory in the presence of Christ, and freedom from their adversary forever and ever. They rejoice eternally that they were on the right side in this mighty conflict.

Here is an old, old question. Why did Almighty God allow Satan to invade the human realm and perpetrate all the deception, devastation and death that have followed in his train? Couldn't He have prevented it all? And if He could have, why didn't He? Some of these questions we might not be able to answer fully, for there is mystery about them, just as there is about so many of God's wise providences. But let's look at some suggestions anyway.

It is certain that God could have destroyed Satan completely and prevented any human encounter with him whatever. Since God had power to cast him and his angels out of heaven and put them into eternal chains of darkness, He could have put them anywhere He chose. Letting them come to the earth and confront the first created human pair was by God's express permission. It didn't happen by accident, or because Satan outwitted God.

Have you noticed that time after time in the Bible, God has challenged Satan and has always defeated him? When Satan tempted Jesus in the wilderness, Satan didn't instigate the encounter; God did. The Spirit led Jesus up into the wilderness to be tempted of the devil. And Jesus won that engagement, not only for Himself but also for us who are often tempted by the devil. In that He suffered, being tempted, He is able to help all others that are tempted. He showed us how to be victorious in temptation and what weapons are effective for the victory: the

Word of God, the fulness of the Spirit, and fervency in prayer. With those weapons Jesus was armed for victory, and we can be also.

When Job had his fierce encounter with Satan's emissaries, it was not Satan who initiated the action. God challenged Satan, asking, "Have you considered my servant Job?" Through a furious and protracted conflict Job was triumphant, and God demonstrated that His power is greater than that of Satan!

This same grand truth was evidenced when God allowed Satan to confront Adam and Eve in the Garden of Eden. We know Adam fell, but, my friend, don't think this means that Satan has outwitted God, or that grace is less powerful than sin. Paul the Apostle takes up this very question in Romans, Chapter 5. And five times in that one chapter he uses the expression "much more" to compare the victory of Christ with the harm done to the race through the fall of Adam. He climaxes the comparison in Romans 5:20 with these words: "Where sin abounded, grace did much more abound." Yes, sin has been a terrible scourge upon the whole human family. Costly—so very costly—was the fall of humanity into sin. But grace has not just barely counteracted the influence of sin. Grace is a "much more" provision for victory! "Where sin abounded, grace did much more abound." In Romans 8:35 Paul listed some of the painful consequences of sin: tribulation, distress, persecution, famine, nakedness, peril, and the sword. Then he exulted, "In all these things we are more than conquerors through him that loved us." We are not just conquerors, mind you; we are more than conquerors! That means we do not just win in this battle; we are made richer by winning than if there had never been a conflict.

I do not understand that completely, and I can not answer all the questions that might arise. But I believe it with all my heart: God's power and glory are going to be magnified far more than if Adam had never fallen into sin. And God will win a colossal victory over Satan! The outcome is already assured, so let us begin to rejoice in the victory!

2

THE HOLY WAR

All of human history is paralleled by an ongoing warfare between God and Satan. Every outbreak of war on earth is an aspect of that conflict in the heavenlies. In most of these conflicts God is on one side and Satan on the other, although sometimes Satan is on both sides. Just like the Communists, who are some of his agents in the earth, he delights to stir up conflicts, and he's willing to be on both sides just to keep them going.

No part of the Bible better surveys the history and issue of this mighty contest than the Second Psalm, which speaks first of David the King, but primarily of Jesus, the Anointed Son of God. One Bible scholar has entitled this Psalm, "The Holy War." It provides an overview of the entire engagement.

THE DEFIANCE OF THE PEOPLE

The Psalm is divided into four parts of three verses each:

- The Defiance of the People (1-3)
- The Derision of the Lord (4-6)
- The Declaration of the Son (7-9)
- The Demands of the Psalmist (10-12)

Here are the Psalmist's words: "Why do the heathen rage, and the people imagine a vain thing? The kings of the earth set themselves, and the rulers take counsel together, against the Lord, and against his anointed, saying, Let us break their bands asunder, and cast away their cords from us" (Psa. 2:1-3). After the ascension of Christ, the apostles applied these verses to the conspiracy of Pilate, Herod, and rulers of Israel, as well as to the Roman authorities, in condemning Jesus to die on the cross. It has a wider application than that, however. It represents a mood that has often been manifested in people of authority who have stood against the truth of God and against holy people who were representing that truth. The passage has its consummate application in the Battle of Armageddon, when the rulers of many nations will join in a march on Jerusalem to abolish God's forces entirely. At least nine books of prophecy in the Bible speak of this battle directly, and others indirectly.

The Psalm begins with a question, "Why do the heathen rage, and the people imagine a vain thing?" The word "heathen" referred just to people outside of Israel—people who did not know God. "Rage" suggests the snorting of a horse as it rushes into battle. The Psalmist asks a very good question: Why are people in general antagonistic to the truth of God? Why don't they gladly submit to His wise government?

The answer is two-fold: because of sin and because of Satan. And ultimately, sin goes back to Satan as its source. Inherited sin—sin of the heart—in its very nature is enmity against God, as St. Paul declares in Romans 8. The sinful heart, until it is touched and changed by divine grace, is in a war against God. It is set against His authority, just like these kings of the earth who said, "Let us break their bands asunder." "Let us refuse His authority, and rebel against His restraints!" That is the spirit which sin generates in the heart.

"Why do the people imagine a vain thing?" the writer continues. That expression "vain imagination" is one which Jeremiah the prophet used often in describing the hearts of the Israelites when they turned away from God and, like their neighbors, bowed down to idols. That imagination, as Jeremiah described it, was not a function of the mind. It came from the heart. The word from the Hebrew literally means a heart that is stubborn, blind, and set against God. That is the problem of the heart. It sets people against God. So until they are regenerated and transformed by God's grace, they are already on the wrong side in this age-old conflict. They are in league with the devil, whether they are aware of it or not.

A second reason for the defiance of the people is the motivation of Satan. The people "set themselves" against the Lord, said the Psalmist. That also indicates a defiant stance. It resembles the posture of Goliath as he shouted his arrogant challenge against God's army in Israel.

Have you ever wondered how the rulers of this world achieve so much unanimity in their stand against righteousness—against moral laws and holy principles? How do educators, media people, and social policy makers gain so much of a consensus when they don't even reflect the wishes of their constituents? The answer is in the Bible! The question asked by the Psalmist relates to the battle of men against God that will finally be expressed at Armageddon. How can the kings and presidents of this world reach agreement to join in an all-out battle against God in Jerusalem? In Revelation 16:13-14, John gives the answer, "And I saw three unclean spirits like frogs come out of the mouth of the dragon, and out of the mouth of the beast, and out of the mouth of the false prophet." (That is the Satanic trinity, the counterpart of the Father, Son and Holy Spirit.) John continued to explain, saying, "They are the spirits of devils, working miracles, which go forth unto the kings of the earth and of the whole world, to gather them to the battle of that great day of God Almighty."

My friend, here is an awesome truth indeed! Satan has power to inject his own thoughts into the minds of men and women. If they have no spiritual discernment, they may well accept his thinking as their own, even congratulating themselves on the brilliance of their ideas.

I want to illustrate this startling truth from the New Testament. Do you remember the case of Ananias and Sapphira? Their story is told in Acts, Chapter 5. When other believers were giving all of their possessions to advance the early church, this couple wanted to get the credit for doing the same, but they did not want to make that kind of sacrifice. So they sold their property but kept back part of the price for themselves. Then they pretended they were giving all to the Lord and His Church. Peter the Apostle, though, had enough spiritual discernment to sense their fraud. Here's what he said: "Ananias, why hath Satan filled thine heart to lie to the Holy Ghost, and to keep back part of the price of the land? . . . Why hast thou conceived this thing in thine heart? Thou hast not lied unto men, but unto God" (vs. 3-4). The word "conceive" here means to design or to purpose something. "Why did you design such a thing?" Peter was asking. You see, Ananias thought it was his own design, but Peter makes clear that Satan introduced the idea into his mind. Ananias received it as his own plan and purpose, acting it out in his fraudulent conduct. He was lying to the Holy Ghost, however, as the Apostle asserted.

It is always Satan's plan to set men against God. At Armageddon kings and generals will unite in warfare against God Himself—all at the clever instigation of Satan, working directly in their minds.

But Armageddon will not be the last battle. Though it will be decisive, there is still a later battle coming. After Satan is released from his thousand-year confinement in the bottomless pit, he will be right back at his same old tactics. Revelation 20:7-8 tells us about it:

> And when the thousand years are expired, Satan shall
> be loosed out of his prison, and shall go out to deceive
> the nations which are in the four quarters of the earth,
> . . . to gather them together to battle: the number of
> whom is as the sand of the sea.

Deception is one of Satan's master strategies in the mind. He projects his own thoughts and false reasonings into human minds and thereby controls entire populations of men. He works through leaders to control their people and through the people to influence their rulers. In it all Satan is seeking recruits for his battle against Almighty God.

Turn back now to Psalm 2. Verse 3 gives the determination of those who are set against God. They say, "Let us break their bands asunder, and cast away their cords from us." The figure is of an ox in harness, being guided with reins controlled by his master. But the ox rebels and decides to tear up the harness, get rid of the restraints, and go his own way.

It is the same spirit which Jesus described in one of His parables about His return to this earth to reign. In Luke 19 He told of a nobleman who went away to gain a kingdom, leaving assigned work for his servants. As Jesus put it, while the man was away his citizens said, "We will not have this man to reign over us."

And when the nobleman returned he punished those disobedient servants with death.

THE DERISION OF THE LORD

We proceed to the second section, verses 4 to 6, which may be entitled "The Derision of the Lord." "He that sitteth in the heavens shall laugh: the Lord shall have them in derision. Then shall he speak unto them in his wrath, and vex them in his sore displeasure. Yet have I set my king upon my holy hill of Zion."

Did you ever hear God laugh? I believe He has a very good sense of humor, but we seldom hear God laughing. Here God laughs, not because of something funny, really, but because of something ridiculous: because of puny men, who actually think they can engage in warfare against the Almighty and win! One reason for laughter is the incongruity of a situation arising when something entirely unexpected and surprising appears. I knew an old Methodist preacher who, as a boy was sent to bed in the attic while the young folks of the community had a taffy party downstairs. That boy felt robbed; he wanted in on the fun also but was considered too young. In his nightshirt he crept out along the joists of the attic to hear what was going on below. In the darkness he suddenly slipped and crashed through the ceiling, landing in the laps of some of the partying girls. Now that was an incongruous situation, and there was laughter aplenty!

It will be something like that when the Battle of Armageddon is concluded. Revelation 19 describes the scene. Kings and captains, warriors and armaments are pressing forward relentlessly to destroy Jerusalem. They are making good progress, too, and are apparently assured of total victory. But then something amazing occurs. Heaven opens, and out rides Jesus on a white horse, followed by His armies on more white horses. And God laughs out loud until the earth is rocked with the sound! The rebels did not expect such a thing as this: *an army from heaven!*

Another reason people laugh is because of the sudden superiority of the one who laughs or the sudden defeat and embarrassment of the proud. When I was in my first year of public school teaching, I took a lanky country boy to the county Field Day in town. He hadn't expected to participate, but when he saw the youngsters preparing to run, he asked if he could join them. Permission was granted, and he proceeded to the starting line. With him was a sizeable group of boys, all in running togs and track shoes. He was dressed in overalls and work shoes. They crouched with their fingers to the ground; he stood upright, rather surprised that they seemed prepared to crawl down the track! Then a gun sounded, and he jumped with surprise. The other boys were off like arrows, while he was recovering from shock. Then he got the idea and started after them. Now he had one decided advantage: he could really run! He was a natural! Before the end of the race he had passed them all and was alone in his victory. There was more than cheering that day: there was laughter—uproarious laughter! The farm boy in work clothes had made the city-trained fellows look sick! He had showed them how to run!

What a day it will be when all the military genius, the high-powered weapons, the throngs of deceived followers of Antichrist are exposed in their folly! They thought they could overcome God and His Christ! How ludicrous they look now! They thought material weapons were the last word in power. They had no time for God. They were determined to be realists, counting just on what can be seen with the eye of flesh. How surprised they are to see Jesus coming in power and glory!

This is not a fairy story, my friend. This is history written in advance. Jesus will one day appear in a dramatic display of authority, bringing a sudden end to this carnal revolt against His Lordship. Paul said, in II Thessalonians 2:8, that when Jesus comes He will consume Antichrist "with the spirit of his mouth, and shall destroy with the brightness of his coming." No shots will be fired; God's army will sustain no injuries. Christ's victory will be achieved by what Paul calls "the spirit of His mouth." In the Revelation John says "out of his mouth goeth a sharp sword." That sword, we know, is His holy Word. Its authority is finally recognized. His enemies now see the truth: Jesus is real after all. He is not just a delusion of simpletons. The brightness of His glory confounds all their plans and nullifies all their resources. He is the Victor!

The outcome of this engagement is that Jesus shall sit upon His throne in Jerusalem and be King over all the earth—forever. "Yet have I set my king upon my holy hill of Zion," is the way the Psalmist expressed it in verse 6.

Satan has desperately resisted the possibility that Jesus might become king in the earth. He has wanted to keep the earth in his own grasp, controlling its population with his deceptions. One of his tactics was to entice Jesus to accept kingship under his authority. In one of the wilderness temptations, Satan offered Him all the kingdoms of the earth if Jesus would just bow down and worship him. Of course Jesus refused. He was not merely seeking a place of authority, although that was rightfully His all the time. He was waiting for God's time and God's method to bring a complete overthrow of Satan's kingdom.

There was a time when Jesus became so popular with the people of Israel that they clamored to make Him king. He still refused, slipping away to a quiet place of seclusion. He was waiting for God's time of total victory. At the Battle of Armageddon that time will have arrived! Satan will be cast into the bottomless pit for a thousand years and all his colleagues will be confronted with judgment before a holy God.

Here is a practical lesson for us. Satan's method is to entice people with *instant gratification*. God's method involves some delays, some self-discipline in suffering and hardship, some patience of faith as we wait for Him to work out His eternal purposes. Satan persuaded Eve in the Garden of Eden to reach for the forbidden fruit. He is still convincing the multitude to grasp at immediate satisfaction rather than to wait and work for the total victory of righteousness in their personal lives and throughout the world.

We should learn well the lesson of Armageddon: those who grasp for power and gratification against the will of God are going to lose everything. Those who submit to God's will may have to endure some privation for awhile. They will often be misrepresented and persecuted. Jesus was also, and we shouldn't fear to follow His leadership. But in the end it will be the followers of Satan who are defeated forever and brought to shame, while the followers of Jesus, clothed in the garments of righteousness, shall follow Him to eternal victory.

What a throng of disillusioned people have been followers of Satan's deception! Eve was driven from the Garden along with her husband, and she lamented, "Satan beguiled me!" Yes, he always does! He promises total fulfilment, but he can never deliver it. He declares that we can resist God and get away with it. But he is going to be defeated, and so are his followers.

Satan persuaded Ananias and Sapphira they could be applauded as sacrificial Christians while being deceitful and self-seeking, keeping part of the money for themselves. They met sudden death as a consequence.

The followers of Jesus will have places of authority and fulfilment forever, not by selfishly snatching at them but by patiently and faithfully serving the Lord. The very last chapter of the Bible, in verses 3-5, describes conditions in the New Jerusalem this way: "And there shall be no more curse: but the throne of God and of the Lamb shall be in it; and his servants shall serve him . . . and they shall reign for ever and ever." "His servants shall serve him." They have been so well satisfied with the Lordship of Christ that they are perfectly happy to go on serving Him in eternity. His service is not an agonizing ordeal but a perfect fulfilment of our human potential.

But notice, "they shall reign for ever and ever," as verse 5 declares. Do you want a throne? Do you long for influence and authority? Do you sense a need of power? God wants you to have all this. You were created for it. But the way to it is through faithful service to God. Satan's method is to bypass service and grab for instant fulfilment. He is going to lose, and you will lose also if you follow his method. You can make a choice and leave Satan's mastery today. Jesus is going to reign forever as King, and you can reign with Him if you will join His army and follow after Him.

THE DECLARATION OF THE SON

The third part of this Psalm, including verses 7 through 9, contains "The Declaration of the Son."

I will declare the decree: the Lord hath said unto me, Thou art my Son; this day have I begotten thee. Ask of me, and I shall give thee the heathen for thine inheritance, and the uttermost parts of the earth for thy possession. Thou shalt break them with a rod of iron; thou shalt dash them in pieces like a potter's vessel.

Here in just three verses is a short sketch of Jesus' human history. We know that Jesus is eternally God, equal with the Father. Here is the history of His Sonship. It speaks of His humanity. When the angel announced to Mary that she was to have a child, and she asked how this could be since she was not married, the angel replied, "The Holy Ghost shall come upon thee, and the power of the Highest shall overshadow thee: therefore also that holy thing which shall be born of thee shall be called the Son of God" (Luke 1:35). So this designation, "the Son of

God," focuses on the virgin birth by which God became man as a factor in His plan for the atonement.

The term "Son of God" focuses also on Jesus' suffering and death by which we are delivered from sin and given spiritual life. In I John 4:9 and 10 we read,

> *In this was manifested the love of God toward us, because that God sent his only begotten Son into the world, that we might live through him. Herein is love, not that we loved God, but that he loved us, and sent his Son to be the propitiation for our sins.*

The word "propitiation" means a satisfaction. By sending His Son to take our sins upon Him, God's justice is satisfied though He grants us forgiveness instead of demanding punishment. Instead of certain, eternal death, we gain eternal life by believing on the Son. As John said, "God sent His Son that we might live through Him."

The resurrection is also included in the concept of the Son of God. In Romans 1:4 St. Paul wrote that Jesus was "declared to be the Son of God with power, according to the spirit of holiness, by the resurrection from the dead."

One further comment about the Sonship of Jesus: as the Son of God He is now our Great High Priest in the presence of the Father. Hebrews 4:14-16 assures us, "Seeing then that we have a great high priest, that is passed into the heavens, Jesus the Son of God, let us hold fast our profession. For we have not an high priest which cannot be touched with the feeling of our infirmities; but was in all points tempted like as we are, yet without sin. Let us therefore come boldly unto the throne of grace, that we may obtain mercy, and find grace to help in time of need."

Do you see what a rich concept this is: *the Son of God?* It means Jesus has put Himself in a position of obedience to His Father so He can be fully identified with us in our humanity and become our Savior.

We are still talking about an ongoing battle between God and Satan. Jesus became man to enter this mighty conflict and to assure victory. In I John 3:8 the Apostle wrote, "He that committeth sin is of the devil; for the devil sinneth from the beginning. For this purpose the Son of God was manifested, that he might destroy the works of the devil." From the time of the fall in the Garden of Eden, Satan has placed his brand [mark] of sin on every new-born child. But the virgin-born Son of God did not have that mark. As the sinless Son of God, He died to meet all the claims of justice against a race of sinners and to remove that mark from all who believe in Him. Thus He destroys the works of the devil.

Now back in Psalm 2, verse 8 promises, "ask of me, and I shall give thee the heathen for thine inheritance." This section begins with reference to a decree which the Son declares. The decree is a covenant between the Father and the Son. The Father appointed His Son to be our Savior by going to Calvary and dying in our place. As a consequence the Son receives promise of a special inheritance. Sometimes we hear this promise used by missionaries as if God were assuring them that they will receive the heathen as their inheritance by going forth to preach His Gospel. While there is some truth in this interpretation, it is not the real meaning of the passage. God was promising an inheritance to His Son. In the Old Testament it is written that Israel is the inheritance of the Father. The Lord of hosts spoke in Isaiah 19:25, saying, "Blessed be . . . Israel mine inheritance." Now the Son is to have an inheritance also if He asks the Father for it. And in His great intercessory prayer, John 17, Jesus did ask the Father for it. He prayed,

> *I have manifested thy name unto the men which thou gavest me out of the world: thine they were, and thou gavest them me; and they have kept thy word. . . . Father, I will that they also, whom thou hast given me, be with me where I am; that they may behold my glory, which thou hast given me" (vs. 6, 24).*

When Israel went forth to war in Old Testament times, the winning captain could take a wife from among the captives if he caused her to be thoroughly purified from all her pagan uncleanness and if she became totally weaned from her parents and her homeland (Deuteronomy 21:10-14). Now Jesus has entered this holy warfare to recover the captives of sin, and He also is permitted to take a wife from among them. Just as Israel was God's inheritance, the Church has become Christ's inheritance. St. Paul was writing a kind of wedding song when he said, "Husbands love your wives, even as Christ also loved the church, and gave himself for it; that he might sanctify and cleanse it with the washing of water by the word, that he might present it to himself a glorious church, not having spot, or wrinkle, or any such thing; but that it should be holy and without blemish" (Eph. 5:25-27). The same chapter that tells about a captain taking a captive for his wife also tells about the penalty to be required of a disobedient son who refused discipline: he was to be stoned to death before the elders of the city. Likewise the Second Psalm, which tells of the inheritance of the Son, speaks also of the judgment which shall come upon those who will not submit to His authority. They shall be broken with a rod of iron. God expresses infinite love through His Son, but there is also infinite wrath upon those who refuse His love.

THE DEMANDS OF THE PSALMIST

The Psalm closes with a section entitled "The Demands of the Psalmist." "Be wise now therefore, O ye kings: be instructed, ye judges of the earth. Serve the Lord with fear, and rejoice with trembling. Kiss the Son, lest he be angry, and ye perish from the way, when his wrath is kindled but a little. Blessed are all they that put their trust in him" (vs. 10-12). This is in fact the message of the Church to the world.

It is a message of instruction, "be instructed, ye judges of the earth." The Great Commission of Jesus to His Church is a commission to instruct. He said, "Go ye therefore and teach all nations . . ." Old Testament servants could be trained to become faithful soldiers in the army of their master. We are likewise to instruct sinners so they will become faithful servants of the Lord.

Perhaps all of this seems somewhat ominous and frightful: sinners must submit to Christ as Lord or be broken in judgment. The Psalmist anticipates such a thought, and so he says, "Rejoice with trembling!" It is indeed serious business, either to receive or to reject the Lordship of Christ. But there is joy in making Him Lord. In the midst of great seriousness there is also great joy. Condemnation and conviction for sin can be an agonizing experience, and it ought to be! The consequences of sin are horrible in the extreme. But a sinner who surrenders to the majesty and might of Christ does not find himself facing a formidable tyrant. Rather, he finds joy: the joy of love, forgiveness, fellowship and rewarding service!

"Kiss the Son, lest he be angry," the Psalmist exhorted in verse 12. In Old Testament times, to kiss a ruler was a token both of submission and of honor. So to kiss the Son means to submit to the Lordship of Christ and to place Him in the position of highest honor in your life. The ultimatum given is a gracious one. Jesus wants your love and your willing service. He'll be a wonderful Master, bringing joy and fulfilment into the lives of all His servants. But if you will not respect His love and respond to His mercy, then He will show you His anger and His righteous judgments.

The final note of the Psalm is a benediction. It is true that God will display wrath upon unrepentant sinners, but He prefers to give blessing. The Psalm ends with these words, "Blessed are all they that put their trust in Him." My friend, you can do that today. Be instructed to serve Him. Rejoice in His forgiveness. Pledge Him your eternal loyalty. He's the Victor in the battle against sin and the devil, and you can be on the winning side with Him.

3

ISRAEL, GOD'S ARMY

In the first chapter it was stated that God used Israel as His fighting force in Old Testament times and that He has chosen the Church as His army in this New Testament age. Sometimes God used other forces—angels or even heathen nations—to accomplish His will, but generally Israel was His army. There are instructive parallels between the principles of warfare which God used for Israel and the principles which the Church must follow today to accomplish God's purpose for her. As we proceed, we'll be looking for such principles.

The Bible often speaks of "the armies of Israel." Before His people ever left Egypt God spoke to Moses, as recorded in Exodus 7:4, 5, saying, "Pharaoh shall not hearken unto you, that I may lay my hand upon Egypt, and bring forth mine armies, and my people the children of Israel, out of the land of Egypt by great judgments. And the Egyptians shall know that I am the Lord, . . ." Let me note right here the purpose of God in using His armies. "The Egyptians shall know that I am the Lord," He said. God never uses His armies to magnify themselves, to exalt themselves to high honor. He uses them to show that He is God, that He alone is worthy of honor. That is why He chose an enslaved people who had never been a nation before to be His army. It was not to show their greatness, but His own. God's motive in battle is always to show His own character to the world.

When the tabernacle was completed in the wilderness, the tribes of Israel were encamped as armies around it. In Numbers, chapter 2, the order of encampment is given. Verses 3 and 4, for example, describe the camp of Judah: "And on the east side toward the rising of the sun shall they of the standard of the camp of Judah pitch throughout their armies: and Nahshon the son of Amminadab shall be captain of the children of Judah. And his host, and those that were numbered of them, were threescore and fourteen thousand and six hundred." The terms used in this chapter are military terms: armies, camps, captains, ranks, and standards. Israel was developing into an effective army for God.

Let me give one more example. Many years later, for their sinful failure, God let Israel go into Babylon a defeated and captive army. But He did not forget them there. He determined to bring judgment upon the mighty nation of Babylon and to deliver His people again. In Jeremiah 51 God expressed concern for these captives of His, saying in verses 19 and 23, "Israel is the rod of his inheritance: the Lord of hosts is his name. Thou art my battle axe and weapons of war: for with thee will I break in pieces the nations, and with thee will I destroy kingdoms; . . . and with thee will I break in pieces captains and rulers." God had not forgotten His people; He had only designed to refine them and then to restore them as His effective army once more.

On being returned to Jerusalem they were to sing these words, as given in verse 10, "The Lord hath brought forth our righteousness: come, and let us declare in Zion the work of the Lord our God." This was their purpose from the beginning: to display God's righteousness, and declare before all peoples the work of the Lord. Listen to that refrain again: "Come, and let us declare in Zion the work of the Lord our God." That is just like the infant Church as it came forth from the upper room on the day of Pentecost. Acts 2:11 says they were all speaking "the wonderful works of God." And that is still the purpose of the Church today!

GOD'S PURPOSE FOR HIS ARMY

God had three special purposes for His army of Israel when they occupied Canaan as their homeland.

First, they were to destroy the wicked nations that dwelled in Canaan before them. The cup of iniquity was now full for those pagan peoples. Their idolatry, their immorality, their dreadful infectious diseases—a consequence of their sinful style of living—made them worthy of death, and God assigned to Israel the task of destruction. Here is the order God gave, in Deuteronomy 7:16, "Thou shall consume all the people which the Lord thy God shall deliver to thee; thine eye shall have no pity upon them: neither shalt thou serve their gods; for that will be a snare unto thee."

Does the Church have a task like that? Is there a parallel here? Of course, the Church is not commanded to kill everybody who is wicked in the sight of God. One time James and John wanted to call down fire from heaven to consume their adversaries, but Jesus rebuked them, saying, "The Son of man is not come to destroy men's lives, but to save them" (Luke 9:56).

There is, nevertheless, a strong parallel to the Church here. The land of Canaan was a special place prepared of God where He could dwell among His people. In Zechariah 2:12, the prophet said, "the Lord shall inherit Judah his portion in the holy land, and shall choose Jerusalem." The land of promise is called the holy land. It was a place set apart for a holy people. Canaan is not a type of heaven, as some people have claimed. Rather, it is a type of spiritual rest and victory which the Church is to find through Jesus Christ, the Hebrew writer so strongly insists in Chapter 4 of his epistle. The heathen tribes which had dwelled in that land are types of sinful character traits that are to be destroyed from the hearts of God's people so they can enjoy His perfect peace.

Names of those tribes have meanings which are very significant in this regard. Here are some of them, as found in Numbers 13:29. "The Amalekites dwell in the land of the south: and the Hittites, and the Jebusites, and the Amorites, dwell in the mountains: and the Canaanites dwell by the sea, and by the coast of Jordan." You may recall that Amalek was a grandson of Esau, the twin brother of Jacob. St. Paul took Esau as a type of the flesh, and Amalek was of the same disposition. His name means "warlike." Wherever *Amalekites* confronted Israel, they always were at war, seeking to defeat and hinder God's army. That is exactly the character of sinful lusts today: they war against the soul.

The word *Hittite* means terror or fear. This is one of the most common traits of a sinful heart: the fear to witness, the fear to be set apart from the world and be different from it, the fear of death, and many other fears. "He that feareth is not made perfect in love," wrote the Apostle in I John 4:18. And he added, "Perfect love casteth out fear."

The *Jebusites* were a third group. Their name means to be polluted and trampled under foot. It signifies uncleanness, defeat, and slavery. Jebus, the stronghold of the Jebusites, was later to become Jerusalem, the city of peace. What a transformation, when defeat is exchanged for peace and victory!

The term *Amorite* means one who seeks publicity and prominence. That was the characteristic of Jesus' own disciples before they had their Pentecost; afterward they were humble, and willing to serve their Master.

The children of *Anak* were giants who were a real fright to Israel. The name means to adorn with a necklace that chokes the wearer. It represents all those types of adornment that are inconsistent with spiritual life and breath.

Finally, the word *Canaanite* means to humiliate and to overcome. Those Canaanites never compromised. They had to be defeated or they would defeat God's people. Sin is just like that, my friend. Those sinful traits in the human heart have the seeds of defeat in them. They must be destroyed if God's Church is to abide in spiritual rest and victory.

It is this analogy between the pagan tribes in Canaan and sin in the human heart which the writer stresses so strongly in Hebrews, Chapters 3 and 4. He reminds us how Israel came to Kadesh Barnea and refused to go into the promised land because they feared the tribal warriors there. Then he applies the analogy to Christians: "Take heed, brethren, lest there be in any of you an evil heart of unbelief, in departing from the living God. . . . lest any of you be hardened through the deceitfulness of sin" (vs. 12-13). There is a sin problem in the heart, and it requires radical destruction, just as those pagan tribes did.

Do you remember how God said He would help Israel remove all those warring tribes? In Deuteronomy 7 He said, "Thou shalt not be afraid of them . . . the Lord thy God will send the hornet among them, until they that are left, and hide themselves from thee, be destroyed" (vs. 18, 20). Every hidden Hittite and Jebusite would have a swarm of God's hornets searching him out. And not even a giant of Anak could stand against those sharp stingers! Out of their hiding places they would come in a hurry, and the Israelites could then pick them off! God has a similar weapon today. Hebrews 4:12 explains it: "The Word of God is quick and powerful, and sharper than any two-edged sword, [yes, sharper than hornet's stinger! And this Word] is a discerner of the thoughts and intents of the heart," the writer declares. That is where sin is located, in the thoughts and intentions of the heart. But the Word of God can search out the sin, and the blood of Christ can cleanse it away. So shall the Church become God's true fighting force.

The second special purpose of Israel was to make God known to the pagan world as the true God—the God of power and holiness. When Israel came to Mt. Sinai after their deliverance from Egypt, God spoke to them just before giving them the Ten Commandments and said, as recorded in Exodus 19:5-6, "If ye will obey my voice indeed, and keep my covenant, then ye shall be a peculiar treasure unto me above all people: for all the earth is mine: and ye shall be unto me a kingdom of priests, and an holy nation."

Look at that relationship more closely. God said they were to be a holy nation. That word "holy" means to be set apart to a special purpose, but it also means to be pure in conduct, righteous in character and disposition. They were to keep the commandments faithfully. Whenever they sinned, they were to make thorough confession, offering the required sacrifices for sin and making full restitution, too. They were not ever to treat sin lightly! God required a holy people!

Moreover, He said they were to be a kingdom of priests. The priest was a special person who could go into the presence of God, representing the people, and then go out to the people representing God. Israel was to be a kingdom of priests. That means as a people they were to have immediate access to the presence of God. He would dwell among them in a humble tabernacle built for the purpose, and they could come near unto Him. But that was not all. *They were then to go out and represent God before all the other nations of the world.* They were not given these rich privileges of access to God just to keep to themselves and to become proud and exclusive. They were to make God known to all the world! That was their high purpose as a special nation before God—to reveal God's character to other people.

That is exactly the purpose of the Church today. In fact, Peter took this very passage and applied it to the early Christians. In I Peter 2:9-10 he wrote,

Ye are a chosen generation, a royal priesthood, an holy nation, a peculiar people; that ye should show forth the praises of him who hath called you out of darkness into his marvelous light: which in time past were not a people, but are now the people of God: which had not obtained mercy, but now have obtained mercy.

This is a message for the Church. They weren't a people in Old Testament times. Israel was God's special people then, but the Church is today. And like Israel, the Church is a holy priesthood. Peter says the Church's purpose is to "show forth the praises of him who hath called us out of darkness into his marvelous light." *We all are something, that we should all do something.* We must never forget that! We are a royal priesthood, that we should show forth the praises of Christ! If ever we clutch our special blessings to ourselves as if we are just more valuable than other people, we risk being set aside, just as Israel was set aside when they became selfish and exclusive about their privileges.

Yes, Israel was to make God known by their CHARACTER. But they were also to make Him known by their CONQUESTS. Against far superior military forces they were always assured of victory if they would faithfully obey God's commandments, in order that the defeated nations would know it was GOD'S victory. This little rag-tag army, just coming out of forty years of wandering in the wilderness, surely did not rate among the military forces of the world. But they were God's army, and He intended always to give them the victory in order that all men could see that His weapons are not carnal. He does not win with sword and spear but with His own choice of weapons that illustrate His wisdom and power. We will be looking at some of these weapons later: a small stone from David's sling, a donkey's jawbone in the hand of Samson, the pitchers and trumpets of Gideon—these and many more. Israel was never meant to shine as a mighty power in their own strength but to magnify the supernatural power of God!

The book of Deuteronomy was written just before Israel went into Canaan. In Chapter 28 God reviewed the rich blessings that would come to them if they faithfully obeyed His law, and He also told them the terrible plagues and curses that would come to them if they failed to obey. Here is a summary of some of the blessings, in verses 7 to 10:

> *The Lord shall cause thine enemies that rise up against thee to be smitten before thy face: they shall come out against thee one way, and flee before thee seven ways.*
> *... The Lord shall establish thee an holy people unto himself, as he hath sworn unto thee, if thou shalt keep the commandments of the Lord thy God, and walk in his ways. And all the people of the earth shall see that thou art called by the name of the Lord; and they shall be afraid of thee.*

Do you see it? They would always have victory, so all the people of the earth would know they belonged to God and the victory was His.

That reminds me of the passionate prayer of Jesus, just before He went to Calvary. In John 17:18-21, He prayed this way for His disciples:

> *As thou hast sent me into the world, even so have I also sent them into the world. And for their sakes I sanctify myself, that they also might be sanctified through the truth. Neither pray I for these alone, but for them also which shall believe on me through their word; that they all may be one; as thou, Father, art in me, and I in thee, that they also may be one in us: that the world may believe that thou hast sent me.*

Jesus wanted His people to be sanctified; He wanted them to be one, that the world might believe in Him! Ah, that is our purpose for being here: we are to be sanctified, and we are to be one, but these are not ends in themselves. *The high purpose is to make Him known as the Saviour sent from God to all the world!*

I'm reminded also of the testimony of St. Paul in one of his times of disappointment. Even this courageous apostle had some human frustrations. He had arrived at Troas, and God had opened a door for Gospel ministry there. But Titus did not arrive on schedule, and Paul was frustrated. In II Corinthians 2:13 and 14 he tells about it: "I had no rest in my spirit, because I found not Titus my brother: but taking my leave of them, I went from thence into Macedonia." He had to leave God's open door and go hunt a tardy helper! That sounds like some of our problems, doesn't it? But Paul did not start quarreling and complaining. Here is what he said: "Now thanks be unto God, which always causeth us to triumph in Christ, and maketh manifest the savour of his knowledge by us in every place."

In these and the following verses Paul was using the figure of a Roman victory march, after a military conquest. The Apostle was saying in effect, "I have had a disappointment, and my plans have been changed, but this is not my battle; it is God's battle, and He always wins His battles. Thank God for the victory even when I face a disappointment!" And did you notice the outcome of this victory? The knowledge of Christ is made manifest in every place. That was the purpose of Israel's battles, and it is the same with God's Church. We are to make Christ known in all the earth!

The third purpose of Israel was to bring other nations into submission to the law of God. God's instructions are given in Deuteronomy Chapter 20. He made a distinction between foreign nations and those that dwelled in Canaan. The latter were to be totally destroyed, but the nations afar off were to be treated differently. In Deuteronomy 20:10 and 11 God said, "When thou comest nigh unto a city to fight against it, then proclaim peace unto it. And it shall be, if it make thee answer of peace, and open unto thee, then it shall be, that all the people that is found therein shall be tributaries unto thee, and they shall serve thee." He continued by saying that if the far-off city should come forth in battle, Israel would win, and the fighting men of the enemy city would be thoroughly defeated.

The ministry of the Church is like that. Within the circle of her own dwelling she is to be pure from sin. There must be no truce with it. But she, like Israel, is to go forth to those who are bound in sin and give them an offer of peace. When Jesus sent His disciples on their first missionary journey He told them to approach each city and house with a message of peace. If the house responds peaceably, let your peace abide there, He said. But if they refuse it, let your peace depart; it will be better for Sodom and Gomorrah than for that city, in the day of judgment! Likewise the Church today bears a message, and when men reject it they are inviting judgment.

GOD'S REQUIREMENTS FOR HIS ARMY

We have observed God's purposes for Israel; next we want to look at His requirements for Israel if she were to continue serving effectively as His army. They also have their parallel in the Church.

The *first requirement* was obedience to His laws, which were given to them for their good. Before Israel entered Canaan, Moses gave the law to them a second time, as recorded in Deuteronomy 6:24-25: "The Lord commanded us to do all these statutes, to fear the Lord our God, for our good always, that he might preserve us alive, as it is at this day. And it shall be our righteousness, if we observe to do all these commandments before the Lord our God, as he hath commanded us." Again in Deuteronomy 28:9-10 a similar exhortation is given:

> *The Lord shall establish thee an holy people unto him-self, as he hath sworn unto thee, if thou shalt keep the commandments of the Lord thy God, and walk in his ways. And all people of the earth shall see that thou art called by the name of the Lord; and they shall be afraid of thee.*

Observe, please, that the law was not an impossible requirement, not an unreasonable imposition by a God who just wanted to make His people fall. It was given to them for their good. It would be their righteousness if they would walk in it. In this wonderful book of Deuteronomy, God gave His people promises of almost unbelievable blessings if they would carefully keep His law, and equally remarkable threatenings if they refused to obey it.

When Israel did obey His law, God gave them tremendous victories over their enemies just as He said He would. Jericho fell before them, and Makkedah, and Libnah, and Lachish, and many more cities. But when they disobeyed they suffered defeat. Ai was one of those places, and Beth-shean, and Megiddo, and others. Israel stopped short of complete victory, allowing some of the enemy to survive. And those remaining enemies began to multiply and cause real problems. Here is a summary of their plight, in Judges 2:20-22,

> *The anger of the Lord was hot against Israel; and he said, Because that this people hath transgressed my cov-enant which I commanded their fathers, and have not hearkened unto my voice; I also will not henceforth drive out any from before them of the nations which Joshua left when he died: that through them I may prove Israel,*

whether they will keep the way of the Lord to walk therein, as their fathers did keep it, or not.

And finally Israel was taken away into Babylon as slaves, because they would not keep God's commandments faithfully. They were meant to be missionaries to other nations, but instead they became slaves—just because they would not keep God's wise commandments for their own good.

What a lesson there is for us here! The Church is also to keep God's commands. My friend, let no one persuade you otherwise. While we are certainly not saved by keeping the commands of God's law, we cannot be saved and remain faithful followers of God without keeping those commandments. Jesus said, "If ye love me, keep my commandments" (John 14:15). And again He said, "He that hath my commandments, and keepeth them, he it is that loveth me . . ." (John 14:21). St. John wrote, "This is the love of God, that we keep his commandments: and his commandments are not grievous" (I John 5:3). So you see, *it is impossible truly to love God if we aren't keeping His commands.*

Somebody may say, "But we know it is impossible to keep His commandments anyway, and we are no longer judged by law-keeping, but by our trust in Christ as our Savior." It is true, of course, that nobody in his natural, sinful state can perfectly keep God's law. Paul said of the carnal mind that "it is not subject to the law of God, neither indeed can be" (Rom. 8:7). That is exactly why there has to be a deliverance from the carnal mind. The problem is not in human ability when aided by the Spirit of God; the problem is in human motivation. Sin involves a depravity of our motives, so that carnal people do not deeply desire to keep the law of God. But God has cleansing for our desires; He has correction for fleshly motivation. The "carnal mind" is simply the minding of the flesh instead of the Spirit, and that perversion can be corrected. In God's new Covenant He writes His law on our hearts, so we can say with the Psalmist, "I delight to do thy will, O my God: yea, thy law is within my heart" (Psa. 40:8).

A second requirement for Israel was separation from the pagan nations around them. In Deuteronomy, we have this warning in Chapter 7 with reference to the defeated nations in Canaan,

Thou shalt make no covenant with them, nor show mercy unto them: neither shalt thou make marriages with them; thy daughter thou shalt not give unto his

*son, nor his daughter shalt thou take unto thy son. For
they will turn away thy son from following me, that they
may serve other gods: so will the anger of the Lord be
kindled against you, and destroy thee suddenly (v. 2-4).*

St. Paul takes the same principle of separation and applies
it to the Church of God. In II Corinthians 6:14ff he exhorts,

*Be ye not unequally yoked together with unbelievers:
for what fellowship hath righteousness with unrighteousness? . . . Wherefore come out from among them,
and be ye separate, saith the Lord, and touch not the
unclean thing; and I will receive you, and will be a
Father unto you, and ye shall be my sons and daughters, saith the Lord Almighty. Having therefore these
promises, dearly beloved, let us cleanse ourselves from
all filthiness of the flesh and spirit, perfecting holiness
in the fear of God.*

In I Corinthians 10, Paul told how some of the Israelites were
overthrown in the wilderness because they violated the laws of
separation, and he says, "Now all these things happened unto
them for ensamples: and they are written for our admonition, upon
whom the ends of the world are come" (v. 11).

So the Church of today, just like Israel of old, must be obe-
dient to His laws, and must remain carefully separated from the
lusts of this present world if she is to be an effective army for
the Lord.

The *third requirement* was spiritual empowerment. God knew
that Israel was not sufficient in herself to win the necessary victories over those heathen armies and remain free. So He assured
them, "Thou shalt not be affrighted at them: for the Lord thy
God is among you, a mighty God and terrible. And the Lord thy
God will put out those nations before thee . . ." (Deut. 7:21-22).
It would be *His presence* and *His power* that would make them
continually victorious. They were never to trust in their own ability, or the force of their armies, but in the Lord their God.

When they were headed for captivity in Babylon, the prophet
Isaiah explained the reason, and followed it with a promise. He
gave these words from the Lord:

*Thy first father hath sinned, and thy teachers have
transgressed against me. Therefore I have . . . given*

Jacob to the curse, and Israel to reproaches. Yet now hear, O Jacob my servant; and Israel, whom I have chosen: . . . For I will pour water on him that is thirsty, and floods upon the dry ground: I will pour my spirit upon thy seed, and my blessing upon thine offspring. . . . Fear ye not, neither be afraid: have not I told thee from that time, and have declared it? ye are even my witnesses (Isa. 43:27-44:8).

Israel had failed miserably, but God promised them restoration; He promised them power and victory so they could again be what they were called to be from the beginning: witnesses to the nations.

Let me say it again: *these are lessons for the Church.* Perhaps you have been called of God to be a witness to His power and grace. But you have failed; you have not carefully kept His commandments. You have neglected your separation from the world, and the power of God's Spirit is gone from you. You may be still trying to work for God, but there is no victory, no sense of power and effectiveness. Listen to this word: "I will pour water upon him that is thirsty, and floods upon the dry ground. . . ." There is restoration for you, my friend. Are you thirsty for grace and power from God? Then bow before Him and tell Him so. He waits to be gracious, to pour His forgiveness and renewing grace upon you. In the name of Jesus, you can become effective again. Renew your vow to obey God carefully. Keep yourself in God's grace and separate from the corruptions of this world. You can know once more the fulness of His blessing, and you will be an effective soldier in God's great Army.

4

THE CHURCH, GOD'S ARMY

Having considered the subject, "Israel, God's Army," we now begin on the theme, "The Church, God's Army." In this age the Church is God's army to carry out His spiritual warfare against the powers of darkness. In Ephesians 6:10-12 we read St. Paul's description of this spiritual warfare:

> Finally, my brethren, be strong in the Lord, and in the power of his might. Put on the whole armor of God, that ye may be able to stand against the wiles of the devil. For we wrestle not against flesh and blood, but against principalities, against powers, against the rulers of the darkness of this world, against spiritual wickedness in high places.

There are three important considerations in these and the following verses:

- The Spiritual Opposition (12)
- The Spiritual Armor (13-17)
- The Spiritual Conflict (18-20)

THE SPIRITUAL OPPOSITION

First, let us consider the spiritual opposition we face. The terms that are used in verse 12—principalities, powers, rulers—are called by Weymouth (*The New Testament in Modern Speech*), "the despotisms, the empires, the forces that control and govern this dark world, the spirited hosts of evil arrayed against us in the heavenly warfare." In other words, they are political and military forces in the spirit realm. They are the highly organized demonic forces that are arrayed against God and His Church. Our real battle is not against people—flesh and blood—but against the armies of Satan. These terms which St. Paul uses denote ranks of official leadership, just as different ranks of military officers lead armies, squadrons, battalions and platoons in our nation's military forces.

Operations of Satan's forces are in "the darkness of this world," Paul says. Satan and all his hosts have been placed in everlasting chains of darkness, the Bible tells us, and their effort is to keep everybody else in spiritual darkness also. In II Corinthians 4:4 the Apostle said, "the god of this world hath blinded the minds of them which believe not, lest the light of the glorious gospel of Christ, who is the image of God, should shine unto them." His perpetual effort is to hinder the outreach of gospel light and to hold earth's multiplied millions in the darkness of unbelief.

My dear friend, let us never forget that *this present world is captured and controlled by Satan*. St. John said the whole world is in the power of the evil one. If we become friends of the world, settling down as if our permanent residence were here, setting our goals and deriving our satisfactions strictly in terms of earthly things, then we are losing our effectiveness as Christian soldiers, and we are in danger of losing our souls as well.

When American soldiers have fought on foreign battlefields, they have frequently been enticed by some seductive siren to fraternize with the enemy and compromise their position as defenders of the USA. Satan is working the same art in his efforts to weaken the Church and to prevent the outreach of gospel light. And I remind you, this is a battle of light against darkness. Our task is to penetrate the enemy's ranks with God's light and to rescue those who are bound in Satan's darkness. St. Paul said, in Romans 13:12-14, "The night is far spent, the day is at hand: let us therefore cast off the works of darkness, and let us put on the armor of light. Let us walk honestly, as in the day . . . But put ye on the Lord Jesus Christ, and make not provision for the flesh, to fulfil the lusts thereof." Did you get the force of that?

We are to put on the Lord Jesus Christ. That means we are to be clothed with His very character. We are to put off such things as revelling and drunkenness, indecency and sexual promiscuity, quarreling and jealousy. We are soldiers of light, and we dare not compromise with darkness!

In the American Civil War, we are told, there was a man who wanted to be on both sides in the battle. So he wore a Confederate jacket and Union trousers. As a result the Yankees shot him in the chest, and the Rebels shot him in the legs. When he died neither side wanted to bury him, for both sides considered him a traitor.

But today there are many people who are trying to be on both sides in this spiritual battle. They want to be considered Christians, but they are friends of this world also. They live by the world's standard of values, gratify themselves with the world's amusements, and seek to treasure up the world's wealth. They are not laboring to rescue friends and neighbors from the world's darkness. Instead they are adjusting themselves to the dark— learning to live like moles when they ought to be soaring like eagles!

This is a call to the colors! Put off the works of darkness, and put on the armor of light! Put on the character of Christ!

Ephesians 6:12 says that these satanic spirits operate "in the heavenlies." They surround us by the millions, as prevalent as the very atmosphere. One man of Gadara was infested with a legion of them, which may have been as many as 5,000! Jesus set the man free, and made him into a light bearer who evangelized ten cities! The Church is in a military operation to do the same thing: *to change the slaves of darkness into soldiers of light!*

The armor of God is to be employed so we can stand against "the wiles of the devil." What does that mean? What are the "wiles of the devil?" The word "wiles" means "cunning methods." Do you realize how cunning Satan really is? Do you remember that he brought down into sin the first man—the perfect man— Adam? He brought down the wisest man, Solomon; the strongest man, Samson; the man after God's own heart, David; and two of Jesus' own disciples, Judas and Peter. That is not the end of the list, of course, but a sample to show how cunning and powerful a foe he is. You and I are constantly confronted by this cunning adversary, and unless we have on the armor of God, we are not equal to his devices.

Satan's aim is to oppose Christ, to rule this world, and to keep people in spiritual darkness. Just look at his success today! More than half the world is still locked in spiritual darkness, without a vital witness to the saving merits of Christ. Those men and women, boys and girls, who are trapped in the darkness of sin are the trophies to be won in "Operation Outreach"—the spiritual warfare of the Church!

Let us look for a moment at some of the cunning methods the devil uses to captivate and control his millions in the earth. Surely *deception* is a primary one. St. John declared that this "old serpent" deceiveth the whole world (Rev. 12:9). He injects his false ideas into the minds of men, and they accept them as their own— thinking themselves wise to entertain such notions!

Let me give you an example. I recently met a young man who had been on drugs from the age of 12 to 20. He told me that life for him had become supremely miserable, since he had to plan crimes almost daily to get money for his vicious habit. He had met some professed Christians, who told him he needed Jesus. But the next day he saw them at the same drug outlet where he was getting his supply. He concluded Christians were fakes. A bit later he was invited by a pastor's daughter to visit the parsonage, where he was enticed into immorality. His opinion was reinforced: all Christians were phoneys! Now that is the reasoning of Satan: take two examples of hypocrites and conclude that all Christians are fakes! Not even the devil could persuade you that all college graduates are doctors, just because you have met two that are. But he can persuade a multitude, just with two or three examples, that every Christian is a hypocrite. That is his business, to deceive people.

I am glad to tell you that this young man found some real Christians, some people who showed him love and the Spirit of Christ. Today he is a follower of Jesus, and he has discovered that the real fraud is the devil himself!

Discouragement is another method of Satan. Maybe you have tried to be a Christian, and you have failed. And to be sure, the devil has told you there is no use for you to try again. This Christian life just is not for you. It is all right for somebody with better upbringing, somebody who is naturally good, somebody with less opposition than you face; but you cannot make it. Yes, that is one of Satan's main devices: discouragement. But he is a liar— always. Peter became established after repeated failures, and was a leader among the apostles, even writing two New Testament epistles. If he could overcome failure, you can also with God's wonderful grace.

Finally, Satan entices people into bondage with the claim that "one little taste won't hurt you." Just one cigarette, just one drug trip, just one fling into free sex won't hurt you. After all, experiment. And Satan is rejoicing that he has another captive in his snares!

THE ARMOR

Second, let us consider the Christian's spiritual armor. Here is St. Paul's description of it in Ephesians 6:14-17,

> *Stand therefore, having your loins girt about with truth, and having on the breastplate of righteousness; and your feet shod with the preparation of the gospel of peace; above all, taking the shield of faith, wherewith ye shall be able to quench all the fiery darts of the wicked. And take the helmet of salvation, and the sword of the Spirit, which is the word of God.*

Let us notice the pieces of that armor. The first to be put on was the girdle or *belt of truth*. The soldier used this to tuck in his loose-fitting garment and to secure other parts of the armor as well as to hold his sword, much as officers have their pistols secured with a holster and belt today. This represents the truth, Paul says. In the fight against satanic error, truth is absolutely fundamental. Unless a person is totally committed to it, he will be ineffective in spiritual conflict.

God's universe is built on truth and not error. Truth is involved in the very fabric of the moral world. It is not something tentative or optional; it is as definite and unchangeable as scientific laws are. The law of gravity is not an arbitrary notion; it is a principle built right into the structure of the universe. And moral truth is the same. Truth is always in harmony with itself. That is why it can endure forever. Error contains within itself the seeds of its own destruction. It contradicts itself sooner or later, and it cannot endure forever. A bookkeeper may get by for awhile with concealed errors. But sooner or later a careful audit will reveal the discrepancies, and they will not be removed until every error is acknowledged and corrected. My friend, that is how it is with moral error. There has to come a time of reckoning when truth will prevail over error. God's judgment day will be that time of moral reckoning.

Now God's soldiers are to fight *with* the truth and not *against* it. You may recall the case of Achan, a soldier in Israel at the battle for Jericho. Against God's expressed commands, Achan secretly took some of the forbidden silver and goods of Jericho. Nobody else saw him take it, and he had it safely hidden away. But God commands His own army, and He saw the duplicity. He would not let it pass. He let the whole nation suffer humiliation in the next battle until the error was openly confessed and punishment was administered.

David the Psalmist prayed, "Behold, thou desirest truth in the inward parts: and in the hidden part thou shalt make me to know wisdom. Purge me with hyssop, and I shall be clean: wash me, and I shall be whiter than snow" (Psa. 51:6-7). He had covered up awful sin for awhile but endured misery and failure until, before God, he confessed fully and accepted the due retribution for his sin.

My friend, do you claim to be one of God's soldiers? Are you in this battle of truth against error—of light against darkness? Then you must have the girdle of truth. If you are covering up secret dishonesty, unconfessed sins, or moral inconsistencies, you are not ready to fight in God's army! God is going to win His battle, for sure! And He is going to do it without compromising with error! Let's be done with subtle dishonesties and shallow compromises! Truth—eternal truth—is built into God's kingdom, and His soldiers must be in harmony with it.

The second part of the Christian's armor is *the breastplate of righteousness*. The breastplate was a defensive device used to protect the vital organs of the thorax from danger. For the Christian this protection is in the practice of righteousness. In Isaiah 59:17 the prophet portrayed the Lord as putting on "righteousness as a breastplate, and an helmet of salvation upon his head." What St. Paul obviously means is that a person who practices unrighteousness is defenseless against the enemy; he has no breastplate. We are not just talking now about what a person believes in his head but what he lives outwardly in his conduct. We are not talking about mere human righteousness either, but the righteousness of God, which He imparts to the believing soul, enabling that person to live in a Christlike way before the world.

The soldier's shoes represent *the preparation of the gospel of peace.* Barefooted soldiers are not effective in battle. They need their shoes on if they are to march over rough ground, carry heavy loads, and stand against a rugged enemy.

The meaning here is that every Christian soldier—and that means every believer—ought to be prepared to present the gospel of peace to somebody in darkness and sin. Probably one of the greatest defects of the Christian Church today is the number of professing Christians who do not know how to lead another person to saving faith in Christ. The gospel is "good news," but if believers do not know how to share that good news they are like barefooted soldiers; they are not able to advance against the enemy.

Every pastor needs to be a "shoe cobbler," preparing his people to deliver the gospel of peace behind enemy lines. Don't forget it, dear friend: the Church is here in this world to take a message of peace to those who are in trouble, a message of deliverance to those in bondage! Are you prepared for that? If not, get your gospel shoes on! Get into the battle for truth! The devil has his ministers all over the world, spreading lies that destroy. How much more should the soldiers of Christ be going everywhere, spreading the truth that saves!

Next comes the *shield of faith.* The Roman soldier carried a large, oval shield in his left hand. It could be moved easily about to ward off the flaming darts thrown by the enemy. This shield of faith may represent several things. It can mean, first, the body of truth which is included in the gospel of peace. Second, it can mean a personal appropriation of gospel truth that brings salvation. And third, it can mean an attitude of confidence in God and His power to give victory. Perhaps all three are involved. We believe the truth; we have trusted in the truth for personal salvation; and we proceed into the battle with firm confidence that God will give us the victory.

Please notice how each of these parts of the armor comes right back to the matter of truth. We must have the truth; we must believe the truth; and we must be changed by the truth. Otherwise we are not ready for the fight. Out of the Korean War came the sad story of thousands of American soldiers who were not strongly committed to their own cause, and they were easy prey for the Communist brain-washers. These men refused to return to their own homeland after the war but rather pledged allegiance to the enemy. That is because they had not been given a faith to fight and die for.

But we Christians have such a faith. We must be ready to die for the truth, for we know that even if we die for it, we shall live again and reign forever with the God of truth.

Fifth in the armor is the *helmet of salvation*. Unless the soldier has his helmet in place he will be easy for the enemy to overcome. His head will be a ready target for swords or spears. Likewise, if the soldier of the cross does not know he has been born from above—does not know all his sins are forgiven—he will be vulnerable in the fight. The attitude of inner confidence gives boldness in the battle. To know we are ready to live or die for Jesus; to know that the moment of death, if it must come, will be the moment of seeing Jesus—this gives us real courage as we face the foe. We are on the winning side!

The last piece of armor is the only offensive weapon: the *sword of the Spirit*, the Word of God. The foregoing parts are defensive. It is certain that God's soldiers need a good defense against the enemy; however, we can never win battles just fighting defensively. Just forsaking sin and keeping clean in our lifestyle will not win the battle of light against darkness. Our business is to go into the realms of darkness and recover those who are taken captive by the devil. We can never do that with just defensive armor. But we have one weapon that is sufficient in the fight. It is God's Word. Jesus overcame the devil in His temptations by using the Holy Scriptures, and we can do the same. Going up from that place of temptation, Jesus went with power to proclaim the gospel of salvation. He had overcome the foe.

Martin Luther found similar strength in God's eternal Word. In his fiery ordeals a song was born—a song of faith and courage—the song, "A Mighty Fortress is Our God." Hear the confident expectation of triumph in these two verses:

Did we in our own strength confide, our striving would be losing,
    . . .
Were not the right Man on our side, the Man of God's own
    choosing.
Dost ask who that may be? Christ Jesus, it is He;
Lord Sabaoth, His name, from age to age the same,
And He must win the battle.

And though this world, with devils filled, should threaten to undo
    us,

*We will not fear, for God hath willed His truth to triumph through
us.*
The prince of darkness grim—We tremble not at him.
His rage we can endure, For, lo, his doom is sure;
One little word shall fell him.

Martin Luther believed the Word of God guarantees the final
doom of our enemy, Satan. And Martin Luther was right. If we
live by the Word of God—believing it, obeying it, using it in the
battle—we are assured of victory.

THE CONFLICT

After writing of the armor, St. Paul wrote of the conflict itself.
He continued,

> *Praying always with all prayer and supplication in the
> Spirit, and watching thereunto with all perseverance and
> supplication for all saints; and for me, that utterance
> may be given unto me, that I may open my mouth
> boldly, to make known the mystery of the gospel, for
> which I am an ambassador in bonds: that therein I may
> speak boldly, as I ought to speak.*

Here is the battle itself, and it consists of two things: prayer
and proclamation. All the armor is just preparation for effective
praying and effective proclaiming of the gospel.

Notice first that this is serious praying. The word "supplica-
tion" is used, and it refers to a commoner coming into the presence of a king with such a pressing need that he must have help.
Trench called it "the mighty utterance of a mighty need." The
petitioner will not be satisfied with mere formalities; he must have
an audience and an answer. So it is with the prayer warrior; he
or she is not merely saying trite phrases but pressing into the
presence of our King to gain an answer.

Second, this is strenuous praying. In verse 12 the Apostle
says, "We wrestle . . . against principalities, against powers,
against the rulers of the darkness of this world." When do we
do that? When we are praying effectively—when we are pressing
through satanic resistance to reach the throne of grace.

Daniel provides us a good example of such praying. For
twenty-one days he had prayed, eating no pleasant food. Probably he took just bread and water, giving himself to strong praying.

You can read the story in Daniel, chapter ten. After three weeks of prayer and fasting, he was touched with the hand of an angel of God, who told him his prayer was heard. He had been resisted by "the prince of the kingdom of Persia," one of the satanic beings whose assignment was to defend the nation of Persia against the purposes of God. God's people were in captivity, and Satan wanted them to stay there. He had his forces in position to confound God's plan for Israel, and he did not want them freed. But Daniel kept praying and was joined in the conflict by Michael, one of the chief princes in God's heavenly army. Soon the prince of Greece would be joining the fight against God, the angel told Daniel, but he could be assured that his prayer was heard and would be answered with the deliverance of his people from captivity.

Yes, my friend, serious praying involves wrestling with demonic forces. By faith we may *rest* in God, concerning our own salvation. But by faith we need to *wrestle* in prayer concerning the deliverance of others who are in satanic captivity. Are you doing any wrestling in prayer?

Third, this is sustained praying. "Watching thereunto with all perseverance . . . for all saints," Paul says. The word "watching" is a military term, meaning to stay awake. When a battle is raging, everything else takes second place. The first requirement is not a comfortable place to sleep but total involvement in the fight. It is assumed that "all saints" are involved in this battle. They are to pray for each other in the common cause of victory. This implies unity of purpose and cooperation in endeavor so the cause of God will not suffer loss.

Fourth, this is Spirit-empowered praying. It is "praying in the Spirit." A message of this kind sounds like nonsense to a person who does not have the Spirit of God. It is the Spirit Who gives us vision into the realm of spiritual reality and helps us sense the importance of real intercession. The Spirit gives guidance in prayer, indicating where the need is and bestowing spiritual burden about the need. He energizes people in prayer, making them effective, as Daniel was. Praying like this is hard work, just as battlefront engagements are severely exhausting. It is easier to play than to pray, and many people do just what is easy to do. But if the battle is to be won, the saints—God's faithful army—must pray in the Spirit.

The second phase of the battle is proclamation. "Pray for me,"

Paul said, "that utterance may be given unto me, . . . to make known the mystery of the gospel." He needed supernatural power to make known a supernatural message. Men would be saved or lost, depending on how the message went forth through him, and that was a most weighty consideration for the Apostle.

It should be for us also. For I would remind you that the proclamation of God's saving gospel is not just the work of a few apostles and evangelists. St. Paul knew his own special responsibility, and he really expected to see the whole world evangelized in his lifetime. But he did not plan to do it all by himself. He went to the great cities with the message and trained the new converts to share the news with their neighbors.

On the farm I used to watch my father set fire to a weedy field, preparing it for plowing. With a torch he ran across the field, setting small fires along the edge. As the wind fanned those flames, they spread and moved along until soon the whole field was burnt. St. Paul had a similar strategy. At Thessalonica, for example, he spent about three weeks, and with great spiritual power he ministered the Word of God. Believers turned from idols to serve God and to look for Jesus in His return to earth. But they did not sit down to wait. They began to evangelize. And when St. Paul wrote his first epistle to them about a year later, they had already spread the Word so effectively over those parts that the Apostle did not need to come back into the area himself. They had done the job in one year! What an effective battle strategy Paul had!

I am not exaggerating that strategy either. Look back in Ephesians, Chapter 4, where Paul writes about the ministry of the Church. He makes it plain in that chapter that every member has a calling, has a gift, and has a ministry. If every member works effectively, he says, the body of Christ will grow upward and outward at the same time. Listen to the exhortation he gives to the believers: "Speak every man truth with his neighbor" (v. 25). That means more than just not telling lies. It means to tell the truth. And he says "the truth is in Jesus" (v. 21). Finally he exhorts in verse 29, "Let no corrupt communication proceed out of your mouth, but that which is good to the use of edifying, that it may minister grace to the hearers." Do you see that, my friend? Everyone is to speak truth to his neighbor, truth which is centered in Christ, and truth that will minister grace to the hearer!

That was Paul's strategy for a growing and effective Church! That strategy will work today!

So here is the twofold ministry of the Church in battle: *effective prayer and effective proclamation.* The Spirit's empowerment is necessary for both. He makes the proclamation bold, convincing, and transforming. Without Him even the Word of God can become a dead letter, as the Apostle asserted in II Corinthians 3:6, "God also hath made us able ministers of the new testament; not of the letter, but of the spirit: for the letter killeth, but the spirit giveth life." Without effective praying, proclamation is a dead letter, and without effective proclamation, praying is a dead end. The two must be united together if the Church is to be victorious.

This twofold ministry is beautifully illustrated in Exodus, Chapter 17. Israel was on the way from Egypt to Mt. Sinai. At Rephidim the Amalekites came out to fight against them. Moses instructed Joshua how to order the battle: "Choose us out men," he said, "and go out, fight with Amalek: tomorrow I will stand on the top of the hill with the rod of God in mine hand." You may recall that when Moses held up his hands toward God, Joshua prevailed on the battlefield, but when Moses wearied and lowered his hands, the Amalekites prevailed. So Aaron and Hur assisted by holding up Moses' hands, and Joshua won a victory over the enemy.

There are preachers today who feel defeated in their ministry because they have no effective force of praying saints supporting their ministry. There are also believers who are discouraged, for they have prayed long for the salvation of sinners, but there is no effective program of proclamation that gets out to where the sinners are. The Church must have both; the battle is twofold. We must have Spirit-anointed prayers and Spirit-anointed proclaimers. With this combination we can win the battle for God and holiness!

5

VICTORY AT DAMASCUS

I srael's battles were literal engagements with pagan, flesh-and-blood enemies, and they used material weapons. Warfare for the Church is primarily spiritual, and our weapons are not carnal but "are mighty through God to the pulling down of strongholds." Nevertheless the battles of Israel involved lessons and principles that are highly important for the Church in her spiritual warfare. Let us now look at some specific Old Testament battles and discover some of those lessons.

We will begin with the first battle recorded in the Bible and will call the engagement "Victory at Damascus." The story is found in Genesis 14.

Lot, Abram's nephew, had moved into the wicked city of Sodom and taken a job as judge in the city. The notable general, Chedorlaomer, king of Elam, had led an alliance of four kings into battle and had conquered five cities and their kings, including Sodom, where Lot dwelled with his family. All the people and goods of Sodom had been carried away as booty, and their prospects were dark indeed. There was no international court of appeal and no binding rule for civil treatment of prisoners.

A man who escaped from the conquered company took the news to Abram the Hebrew, who dwelled at Hebron.

When Abram heard that his brother was taken captive,
he armed his trained servants, born in his own house,
three hundred and eighteen, and pursued them unto
Dan. And he divided himself against them, he and his
servants, by night, and smote them, and pursued them
unto Hobah, which is on the left hand of Damascus. And
he brought back all the goods, and also brought again
his brother Lot, and his goods, and the women also, and
the people (Gen. 14:14-16).

In this intriguing first story of battle, there are the same elements which are involved in the Church's warfare. I want you to see them and appreciate them so your warfare will be effective in the name of Jesus.

First, we examine "God's Purpose in the Battle."

GOD'S PURPOSE

God was certainly involved in this battle, as Melchizedek later expressed it: "Blessed be the most high God, which hath delivered thine enemies into thy hand" (Gen. 14:20). And God's purpose is plain: it was to deliver captives from bondage—captives who were overcome by a force too great for them to resist. Not only Lot's family but also a multitude of other citizens in five cities were forcibly overcome and carried away to be mistreated as beasts, ravished by wicked men, and used as slaves.

My friend, this is the purpose back of God's whole plan of redemption: *to recover slaves from the bondage of sin and restore them to liberty!* Jesus made the fact clear in His first public message in Nazareth, when He read from Isaiah 61, "The Lord hath anointed me to ... proclaim liberty to the captives, and the opening of the prison to them that are bound. . . . This day is this scripture fulfilled in your ears." That was His ministry, and it is the ministry of the Church as well. We are here to open prison doors, to let captives go free. The whole concept of redemption is briefly this: to recover slaves from their bondage. And here is this concept in the very first Bible battle!

I said in an earlier chapter that Satan is always involved in earthly battles, and sometimes he works on both sides. This story is an illustration. In the first phase of the conflict, four kings under Chedorlaomer fought with five kings and overthrew them. Abram was not involved. The battle occurred in the vale of Siddim, which the commentator Wellhausen has called "Demon Valley." Verse 10 of Genesis 14 says the valley was full of "slime pits," and the kings of Sodom and Gomorrah fell there. Only a remnant got away and fled to the mountain.

What a picture this is of the world's battles! Can't you just see these wicked people of Sodom and Gomorrah, so adjusted to their ease and comforts, their sensuality and their selfishness, running in panic before the sweeping armies of Chedorlaomer and falling in the tar pits around the Dead Sea? This is not a battle for virtue or civil liberty; it is a battle for selfish gain, a cruel demonstration of the pagan notion that might makes right. Men sinking in the mire, women and children carried away to a horrid fate: that is the portrait of Satan's battles. He is a destroyer, and the more of God's image he can deface, the better he likes it. He has no mercy! He will debauch our youth, ravish our womanhood, waste our resources, defile everything sacred, and make slaves of every soul possible just because humanity bears God's image, and Satan hates that image. He does not seek to win people because he has any love for them; he only wants them to be divorced from their Creator and to enlist on his side of the battle against God and righteousness.

Most of this world's battles are not God's battles. James asked the question, "From whence come wars and fightings among you? Come they not hence, even of your lusts that war in your members?" (Jas. 4:1). God is not on either side of such battles, just as He was not in that ancient battle. On one side fought Tidal, king of nations, and his name means *fearfulness.* On the other side was Birsha, king of Gomorrah, and his name signifies *wickedness.* Here was wickedness on one side and fearfulness on the other: isn't that like a lot of fighting today? It proves no virtue, and it gains no real good. It simply demonstrates hate and lust and cruelty! The Church should have no part in such warfare! It is not God's kind of battle!

But look at the following phase of the conflict; that is something different. On one side is God's man of faith going forth, not to plunder and make gain but to rescue slaves from bondage and set them free. That is God's kind of battle! He did not come to destroy but to redeem, not to grasp for gain, but to give and enrich others! That must be our motivation too!

Lot is the key man among those slaves. He was Abram's nephew, called his brother in this story. And really, Lot should not have been in this ugly situation at all. He went to Sodom out of selfishness and compromise. Sodom was a wicked city. Ezekiel described its sins as "pride, fulness of bread, and abundance of idleness; neither did they strengthen the hand of the poor and needy. 'And they were haughty and committed abomination before me: therefore I took them away as I saw good,' said the Lord God." Jesus said the last days would be like the days of Sodom. And they surely are! Eating and drinking, buying and selling, planting and building occupy the minds of the masses. And for pleasure the sins of Sodom are more and more common, notably sodomy—called homosexuality today.

Lot should never have gone there! It cost him his wife, some of his children, and his own virtue in the end.

The mood of Sodom is spreading as a subtle plague now. Preoccupation with material things, tolerance of sensual sins, pride and fulness of bread—aren't they common where you live? Relatives and friends of mine are being overcome with them, and do not even notice it is happening! It is a snare threatening all of us, just as Jesus said it would be. Are you being taken in by it? Are you like Lot, getting up in the world, but losing your spiritual discernment while doing so?

The Church has not only the task of saving people from the slime pits of vice and immorality; we must also rescue those who are just settled in Sodom—decent, but deceived; exemplary in some ways, but ensnared nevertheless—taken in by the appeal of earthly things!

Abram was a man of the mountains. The folks of Sodom City would have laughed at him. He seemed so far behind the times, so individualistic, so solitary, so unsocial. But he had a place in the mountains where he met God personally. And the fate of Sodom was in his hands, because he was in God's hands.

Friend of mine, there are multitudes of people around you and me whose fate is in our hands! That is a sober thought, but it is true. The church is not here today to warm up to the world, to pattern after its programs, just to fit in. It is here to deliver those who have fallen into the slime pits of sin and those who are relatives of Abram: nice people with religious roots, but people who have breathed the air of Sodom so long that they are a part of its mood and manner. They can be just as lost in the city as in the slime pit. And the Church must bring deliverance to them all!

ABRAM'S PREPARATION

Next we examine "Abram's Preparation for the Battle." When you know that he took 318 servants of his household and defeated an alliance of four kings under the leadership of mighty Chedorlaomer, you know he must have had some special preparation—and he surely did.

But that has always been the way in God's battles. His forces have appeared outnumbered from the world's perspective. Yet God gets the victory, because He does not depend on carnal resources. It is always a temptation for us to rely on carnal forces, the strength of numbers, financial resources, gifted leadership, and such like when God wants to demonstrate His own wisdom and strength. We face the temptation in every age, as much today as ever before. But it's still true as God told Zerubbabel, "Not by might, nor by power, but by my Spirit, saith the Lord of hosts." I do not belittle human resources; I simply say they are not sufficient for victory. God may use them, but the glory does not go to them; it goes to Him alone. Never forget it!

Look first at Abram's *attitudes*. Here is what Genesis 14:14 says: "When Abram heard that his brother was taken captive, he armed his trained servants, born in his own house, three-hundred-eighteen, and pursued them unto Dan." He had a real *concern* for his brother, Lot, who was actually his nephew. You remember Lot, don't you? He was a tag-along fellow much like "Mary's little lamb:" "And everywhere that Abram went, there Lot was sure to go." He never built any altars of his own; he just looked on at Abram's. He never pioneered any new ventures; he just got rich from cashing in on Abram's blessings. Finally he had so many flocks that the two men couldn't occupy the same pastures. And good old Abram, instead of grabbing the best for himself, gave Lot first choice! You would think Lot, in warm gratitude, would have insisted otherwise. But he did not; he straightway chose the best for himself: the well-watered plain of Jordan, the best pasture-land in the country. From there he moved into wicked Sodom, changed his tent for a house, and got a job as city judge. No more smelly sheep for him! He was moving up in the world.

But Lot was in real trouble, and there was nobody to help but Uncle Abram. Just think of what Abram could have said: "All right, you young upstart; you took the best away from me.

You had no regard for my seniority or my prior rights in Canaan. Now you've made your own bed; just lie in it! When you're ready to crawl back on your hands and knees, I'm ready to listen!" No, Abram did not act that way at all! Do you know why? Because he was God's friend. He was learning the character of His God, and living in the light of it. He was God's leader in the armies of faith! He was learning to wait for God's time, to trust God's wisdom, and to rest in God's promises.

There was no unforgiveness with Abram. He had suffered privation from an ungrateful nephew, but he would not let a grudge poison his life! Abram was too big to become so small, and resentment makes anybody small. He was lifted above unforgiveness by the God Who was His friend!

I am talking about being an effective soldier in God's army. Do you harbor bitterness toward those who have taken the best and served you leftovers? Can you forgive the mean little people who pose as pious while heaping discredit on you? Are you Mr. Greatheart or Mr. Grumble? Can you go on a mission to rescue a person like Lot, unworthy as he is? If you can, then you have God's own Spirit, and you can fight in His army.

Look further, at Abram's *courage* and *faith*. How outnumbered he was! We do not know how many men were fighting under Chedorlaomer's alliance, but they must have surpassed Abram's troops at least 20 to one! Maybe 50 to one. What a lopsided battle! No man reckoning merely on earthly resources would have had any hope of winning. But Abram had a promise. God had said, back in Abram's first days of walking with him, "I will make thee a great nation, and I will bless thee, . . . and I will bless them that bless thee, and curse him that curseth thee." Now is the time to act on that promise. Abram is going on a mission worthy of His God, and he will risk everything on God's promise of blessing.

Abram's promise was not any bigger than ours if we are going forth in Christ's name. "All power is given unto me, in heaven and in earth," Jesus said, "And lo, I am with you alway, even unto the end of the world" (Matt. 28:18, 20). That power is specifically promised to those who go forth in His name. It is ours, if we are carrying out His grand commission.

We have seen Abram's *attitude;* let's look at his *army.* It was made up of 318 servants, born in his house. In other words, they were slaves, and not sons. When I began this study, I jotted down some questions I wanted answered. One was this: "In those ancient battles, could captive slaves be trusted to become soldiers? Or in the heat of battle would they turn traitor and help defeat their masters?" How about God's army? Do His enemies join and fight with Him, or are they too much of a risk? The answer is here in this story. Abram used those who were born in his house! They were servants, but they had no other loyalty! They were born in his house, and they belonged exclusively to him.

In God's army it is similar. His faithful servants are born in His house. And they are more than servants; they are sons! They have been brought out of slavery to another master, but they have become genuine sons in the family. They are not about to betray their Captain.

Is not that vital today? I fear there are many who claim to be in God's army who have not been born in the house. Their loyalty is still to the world from which they have not released their hearts' affection. They do not bring victory to the Church; they are a liability! Their greatest need is to be born in the house—to be born from above.

These servants of Abram were well trained, too. God said of him, "I know him, that he will command his children and his household after him, and they shall keep the way of the Lord, to do justice and judgment." I can think of few greater compliments from the Lord! He trained his household so well that they would all follow the ways of the Lord! Amidst a pagan environment he kept every child going straight with God. What an achievement! They were *trained* servants. That is the same word used in Proverbs 22:6, "Train up a child in the way he should go: and when he is old, he will not depart from it." The word *train* means "to make submissive, experienced, tried and dedicated." That means our children are to become so familiar and accustomed to the right way that they are dedicated to it. We need so much of that in our Christian homes just now: young people who are wholly devoted to righteousness and who are ready to be good soldiers for Jesus Christ.

Finally, observe Abram's attack on the enemy. It involved a fine example of divine wisdom. Verse 15 says, "he divided himself against them, he and his servants, by night." To divide his tiny army did not look wise at all. They were already vastly outnumbered. Did not they need to stay together? You might think so, but it was God's wisdom that was operating. God knew the enemy; He knew what was best. That was a totally new tactic in battle; nobody ever fought that way before. But it worked so well that Oliver Cromwell, the great British general, centuries later, copied Abram's tactic, and it brought him victory, too.

God's wisdom in our battles is absolutely indispensable! We are not warring against flesh and blood but against demonic forces, and they can outwit us any time. We must have superhuman wisdom! No missionary work can succeed without it! The Church is crippled and weak unless God's wisdom is working in her operations. And remember this, God's wisdom often looks entirely foolish to worldly minds. God gives His wisdom to those who are willing to follow it and to give Him all the glory. It is as needful now as it was when Abram went to battle.

There by Damascus the great alliance collapsed, and Abram recovered all the spoil! Lot was set free, with all his family—yes, and all the rest of the captives, also. Victory was complete. Women and children, fathers and mothers, and all the goods, were recovered.

Thank God for our victory in Jesus! We are more than conquerors through His wisdom, His power and His grace. Let us appropriate the principles of Abram and put them to work in God's Church today!

THE KINGS' PROPOSALS

Finally, look at "The Two Kings Proposals," which were made to Abram after his great victory. He was returning with all the people and goods he had recovered in battle when the two kings came out to meet him. One was the king of Sodom; the other, king of Salem.

Here is the proposition of Sodom's king, as found in Genesis 14:21, "Give me the persons, and take the goods to thyself." "Abram, you've won a great victory," he was saying. "I'll let you keep all the spoils you have brought back if you will honor my proposal and allow me to rule again in Sodom over all the people you have recovered."

We must remember an ancient rule of warfare in order to understand this situation: "To the victor belong the spoils." According to that, not only the goods but also the recovered captives were entirely at Abram's disposal. He could do as he liked with them. But here was the king of Sodom acting as if all were his and he was being generous in giving Abram the goods that were already his by right.

That is so much like one of the temptations of Jesus. Matthew 4:8-9 tells the story: "The devil taketh him up into an exceeding high mountain, and sheweth him all the kingdoms of the world, and the glory of them; and saith unto him, All these things will I give thee, if thou wilt fall down and worship me." Of course, all the kingdoms of the world already belonged to Jesus; He was the Creator and sustainer of them all. But here was Satan, the usurper, proposing that if Jesus would just honor Satan's right over them, he would give them all to Jesus at once. Can you see the striking parallel here? The king of Sodom is a clear type of the devil, the god of this world, proposing to give Abram something that was already his by right if Abram would just honor his authority.

Abram's response was as true as that of Jesus. He rejected the offer completely. He said: "I have lifted up mine hand unto the Lord, the most high God, the possessor of heaven and earth, that I will not take from a thread even to a shoelatchet, and that I will not take anything that is thine, lest thou shouldest say, I have made Abram rich." Abram didn't want Sodom's king to have even the slightest control over him, which would have been the case had he accepted that proposal. He rejected the offer totally, not even taking that which was rightfully his.

Jesus did the same. He refused that offer of earthly kingship, knowing that He would one day be king over all the earth without Satan's help. In fact, He would witness the total overthrow of Satan in His own ascension to universal dominion. Likewise Abram would soon see the total destruction of Sodom, with its king, in God's rain of judgment and fire from heaven.

Now, friend, this is not just interesting history. This story contains vital principles of Christian warfare for all of us. Every time we win a great victory in the name of our Lord, the devil will meet us as we return and make a proposition to us. He will compliment us on what a great job we have done, and he will make a subtle offer that seems so reasonable. "Just keep some of the honor for yourself," he will suggest. "Follow my suggestion, and you will soon have fame and wealth from your ministry of the gospel. You have earned it," he says, "so take it and enjoy it!" There are so many people who are falling into that trap! They are turning God's spiritual victories into means for building up their own fame and fortune. One popular Christian author recently came to realize that he not only was becoming a "Gospel star" but also that he was losing his spiritual perceptions. So he took off for most of a year, went alone with God, and regained his sense of authority under God.

There is no way of estimating what God could do through His Church today if He could have all the glory. But the religious system is promoting stars, human stars, very much in the pattern of Hollywood, though in the name of the Lord. Abram would have no part in such a system. He wouldn't take from a thread to a shoe latchet; he would accept what the God of Heaven wanted him to have, but he would not accept Sodom's offer!

A second king, Melchizedek, king of Salem, met Abram also. His response was much different than the king of Sodom's. His proposal was to give all praise to God. Listen to his words: "Blessed be Abram of the most high God, which hath delivered thine enemies into thy hand." "God gets all the credit," Melchizedek was saying, "for it was God that gave you the victory." And Abram so fully accepted that evaluation that he gave tithes of all the spoil to Melchizedek and took not a piece of it for himself.

I am reminded of a word which St. Paul wrote about Abraham in Romans 4:11-12. He said that Abraham is the father of all them that believe, "who also walk in the steps of that faith of our father Abraham." Did you ever try to take the giant steps of a man like Abraham? The Apostle indicates we are all to walk in Abraham's steps and be his children in the faith.

In this story Abram certainly took a big step of faith. He refused to take even the slightest gain to himself from this daring conquest, though he might have claimed it all, according to the custom of the day and according to the offer of Sodom's king. Can we take that kind of step in faith? When God has made us effective in service, will we faithfully give Him every bit of the honor and glory, taking nothing for ourselves? This is a most vital key to even greater victory in the future. If we fail, we will soon be involved in a merely human operation, keeping the name of the Lord but operating without His supernatural power!

You may want to remind me, though, of St. Paul's statement that the laborer is worthy of his reward (I Tim. 5:18). That is true, certainly, and the Church needs to remember this about her ministers. But even St. Paul did not demand this for himself as a right. That was the attitude of Abram, and it should be ours also.

Before concluding this study about "Victory at Damascus,"

I want to give you a peep into the next chapter, Genesis 15. It is really a continuation of the same story. It begins "After these things the word of the Lord came unto Abram in a vision, saying, 'Fear not, Abram: I am thy shield, and thy exceeding great reward.' "

"Fear not" occurs often in the Bible, but this is the first time it is found. Abram knew that those defeated kings might replenish their forces and come to wipe him out, in sheer retaliation for their humiliating defeat. And Abram did not live in a fortress. He moved about in a tent, while his servants watched his flocks and herds. What could he ever do if a rebuilt army came to destroy him? God gave him the answer: "I am thy shield." Abram had risked everything to fight God's battle; now God would fight Abram's battles. He would defend His friend in time of trouble! Is not that a beautiful assurance?

God gave His servant another final promise also: "I am thy exceeding great reward." Abram had not taken even a shoestring from Sodom and its king, and God had taken note of that fact. So He said, "I will be thy reward—thy great reward—thy exceeding great reward!"

We can never understand how great that reward really is until we see Abraham in the kingdom of Heaven. Jesus said to some who were coming short of the kingdom, "There shall be weeping and gnashing of teeth, when ye shall see Abraham, and Isaac, and Jacob, and all the prophets, in the kingdom of God, and you yourselves thrust out" (Luke 13:28). These were the people who played around just outside the door of the kingdom but never got serious about serving the Lord. They will know how much they have missed when they see Abraham getting his reward. And they will wish forever that they had been faithful as Abraham was.

My friend, we are called to be soldiers in God's army today. And God's soldiers do not dare to get entangled in the affairs of this life; they must labor with the supreme goal of pleasing Him Who has called them to be soldiers. All glory goes to our great Captain. Our reward will come from Him, and when we receive it, we will know it is not deserved; it is all of grace. Until that day, let us be good soldiers.

6

WHEN GOD GOES TO WAR

God went to war against Pharaoh of Egypt, because Pharaoh had gone to war against God! Pharaoh thought God was just another little pagan deity, but he found out better. Here is how Miriam expressed it in her song of victory after God brought His people out from Egypt through the Red Sea: "The Lord is a man of war: the Lord is his name. Pharaoh's chariots and his host hath he cast into the sea: his chosen captains also are drowned in the Red Sea." The story is found in Exodus 14, and the song of victory in chapter 15.

The people of Israel had been slaves in Egypt for over 400 years, and their plight was extremely severe. They cried to God for relief, and He heard them. Moses was sent as their deliverer, and the showdown with Pharaoh followed. The contest got more and more intense until in mad desperation the king led his own army into the Red Sea in pursuit of Israel, and the Egyptians were all drowned as the waters came together again and overflowed them.

This victory stood as the standard measure of God's great power until the resurrection of Christ. It is referred to at least 150 times in the Bible.

In this story I want you to see two things: first, "The Vanity of Fighting *Against* God," and second, "The Victory of Fighting *With* God."

THE VANITY OF FIGHTING *AGAINST* GOD

Pharaoh had a number of advantages as he entered this conflict. He had a trained army, equipped with hundreds of chariots and horsemen, and a captain over every chariot. The Israelites, though nearly a million in number, had no arms, were totally untrained in warfare and were a degraded slave people with little or no sense of pride in their heritage and no desire to move to Canaan. Pharaoh's victory over such a motley band seemed absolutely certain.

Moreover, Pharaoh had a stern determination to bring the host of Israel back into slavery. Although a series of ten devastating plagues had brought chaos and death across his land, he was almost insane with desperation to accomplish his own purpose. He would not submit to Moses, or to Moses' God!

Now determination is a valuable character trait, a real gift from God. Indeed, God had given that quality to Pharaoh, but Pharaoh misused it. This fact explains some otherwise mysterious statements about the king of Egypt. In Exodus 9:16, God said to Pharaoh, "For this cause have I raised thee up, for to show in thee my power; and that my name may be declared throughout all the earth." God's raising Pharaoh up refers to the strength of purpose and endurance given to him through all the plagues, enabling him to resist God's will to the end. That ability came from God, and it might have been used in the service of God rather than in battle against Him.

When the Bible says God hardened Pharaoh's heart, the meaning again is that God strengthened him, enabling him to keep a strong will in the midst of adversities. To stand in spite of great hazards and carry a purpose to fulfilment is a noble quality. It is God's gift, I say. But Pharaoh used it in the wrong way, against God, in spite of the increasing proofs that God's power was greater than his own. A final showdown came, as it had to come, to demonstrate that no mortal man can outwit and overcome the Almighty God.

God's aim in this battle, as it was in Abram's battle against Chedorlaomer and his allies, was to release the captives of Israel. The central purpose in God's redemptive plan is just that: to let captives go free from their bondage. He is always moved with compassion when He sees people bound by habits, burdened by destitution, or otherwise battling against insuperable forces. He hears their cries for help, and He draws near to answer.

God's purpose also was to make His own power known to all the earth. As I have said before, these are principles which apply to the Church in her battle against sin: she is to be used of God to set captives free, and she is to demonstrate the power and glory of God in Christ.

Whenever God allows sin to run its course, He does so in order to give a greater manifestation of His own grace and power. He could have destroyed Pharaoh immediately when he refused to release Israel from their captivity. And He could destroy any sinner at once who resists His will; He waits to extend mercy. If that mercy is rejected, the weight of His certain judgment is increasing all the time, as it was with Pharaoh.

In the final climactic conflict between the forces of Christ and Antichrist, Christ is victorious, of course. But because His victory is delayed while Antichrist boasts himself, the magnitude of that victory is all the greater. Here is part of the song of victory, recorded in Revelation 15:2-3:

> *And I saw . . . them that had gotten the victory over the beast, and over his image, and over his mark, and over the number of his name, stand on the sea of glass, having the harps of God. And they sing the song of Moses the servant of God, and the song of the Lamb, saying, Great and marvelous are thy works, Lord God Almighty; just and true are thy ways, thou King of saints.*

As an old chorus says, "The hotter the battle, the sweeter the victory."

Did you notice that expression, "The song of Moses, and the song of the Lamb?" There is an analogy, you see, between that conflict with Pharaoh and this one with Antichrist. Moses was a type of Christ as he led the people to freedom from that cruel bondage and as they witnessed Pharaoh's destruction. Jesus will lead His people as they witness Antichrist's total ruin as well.

THE VICTORY OF FIGHTING *WITH* GOD

When Moses led the host of Israel to the banks of the Red Sea and they found themselves closed in by Pharaoh's army, the people were terrified. They were undisciplined slaves, with no resources for battle. But Moses exhorted, "Fear ye not, stand still, and see the salvation of the Lord, which he will show to you today: for the Egyptians whom ye have seen today, ye shall see them again no more forever. The Lord shall fight for you, and ye shall hold your peace" (Ex. 14:13, 14). "The Lord shall fight for you"— get that promise! He fought *against* Pharaoh, but He would fight *for* Israel. Why is that?

The answer is found in Deuteronomy 7:7-8,

> *The Lord did not set his love upon you, nor choose you, because ye were more in number than any people; for ye were the fewest of all people: but because the Lord loved you, and because he would keep the oath which he had sworn unto your fathers, hath the Lord brought you out with a mighty hand, and redeemed you out of the house of bondmen, from the hand of Pharaoh king of Egypt.*

You see, this victory did not come to the people of Israel because of any innate virtue in them, for they were very low in virtue. In fact, they were some of the most complaining, demoralized people on earth. But God had a promise to keep, a promise made to Abraham years before, that in his seed all nations of the earth would be blessed. This people was Abraham's seed, and God would keep His promise for Abraham's sake.

The victory came also because of God's infinite love for a helpless people. He is always moved by those who want help but who cannot help themselves. He sees all the defeated people today: those overwhelmed by sorrow, by disaster, by destroying habits, and by the guilt of sin. And He is ready to move in their direction, to bring deliverance.

There was one thing Israel had to do to be delivered. They had to obey God. He said to Moses there at the Red Sea, "Speak unto the children of Israel that they go forward: but lift thou up thy rod, and stretch out thine hand over the sea, and divide it: and the children of Israel shall go on dry ground through the midst of the sea" (v. 15-16). If they would do as God said, they could be free. If not, they were in the trap of Pharaoh, and they had no other way out.

That is just how it is with the multitudes who are in Satan's trap today. God has a way out if they will listen and obey His Word. He delights to break the bands of sin, to set the captives free. And the Church, like Moses, has the message of deliverance for those in bondage. Let us not be afraid to proclaim it.

A momentous victory came to this slave people, not through their own virtue or valor but through the love of God for them and their trust in His Word. They went forward by faith when it seemed sheer folly to do so. But in going forward they were delivered, and Pharaoh was destroyed.

I close with a little chorus we learned when we were missionaries in the West Indies:

Church of God, move forward in the power of the Holy Ghost;
Church of God, move forward, for Jesus is ever the same;
Church of God, move forward; we're more than conquerors in His name;
Church of God, move forward in the power of the Holy Ghost.

AMEN!

7

CONFLICT WITH THREE KINGS

W e take up another of the battles in which God's people, Israel, were involved as they journeyed toward their promised land. Forty years of wandering through the wilderness were drawing to a close, and the people were looking forward to reaching their homeland. The route they planned to follow lay up the east side of the Dead Sea and along the Jordan to a point opposite Jericho, from where they would make their invasion.

There was one problem, though—a big problem. Three formidable kings occupied the land east of Canaan. There was Balak, king of Moab, whose land was east of the Dead Sea. North of him, and east of the Jordan, lay the land of Sihon, king of the Amorites. Still farther north, lying east of the Sea of Galilee and on up to Mt. Hermon, was the land of Bashan and its king, Og.

Consider the names of these kings for a moment. "Balak" means an empty waster. "Sihon" means great and bold, and "Og" means giant. These were formidable people, and destructive. They represent the forces of this world that oppose God's people in their pilgrimage. Their standard is bigness and greatness, but spiritually they are empty and vain.

The involvement with these kings was one of the most important Old Testament battles; it is referred to at least 35 times in the Bible. Here are some principles for the Church which are illustrated by the conflict.

PRINCIPLE ONE: PEACEFUL PROCLAMATION

You will find the story in Numbers 21:21-22, "And Israel sent messengers unto Sihon king of the Amorites, saying, Let me pass through thy land." This was not a threat of war; it was a peaceful request for safe passage.

Over and over in the Word, the Church is instructed to make the same approach to the world. When Jesus sent forth His 70 disciples, He commanded them, "Into whatsoever house ye enter, first say, Peace be to this house. And if the son of peace be there, your peace shall rest upon it: if not, it shall turn to you again" (Luke 10:5-6). And St. Paul exhorted, "If it be possible, as much as lieth in you, live peaceably with all men" (Rom. 12:18). That qualifying phrase, "If it be possible," is appropriate, because the world does not generally respond with the same spirit of peace. God's children are peacemakers, not troublemakers, but there is often conflict anyway. And Jesus said it would be so. When He told His disciples to bear a message of peace, He also informed them, "Think not that I am come to send peace on earth: I came not to send peace, but a sword" (Matt. 10:34). If the world is to be at peace with the Church, it must surrender to the claims of Christ as Lord. But to do that requires a radical separation from former patterns of conduct and former relationships. Too many people seem unwilling to pay such a price for real peace.

PRINCIPLE TWO: FREEDOM FROM ENTANGLEMENT

The message to Sihon continued like this: "We will not turn into the fields, or into the vineyards; we will not drink of the waters of the well: but we will go along by the king's high way, until we be past thy borders" (Num. 21:22). Is not that a fitting portrait of the Christian pilgrim? One songwriter put it this way: "This world is not my home; I'm just passing through; My treasures are laid up somewhere beyond the blue. The angels beckon me from Heaven's open door; and I can't feel at home in this world anymore."

This principle also is repeated over and over in the Bible. Jesus was speaking especially of the last days when He warned, "Take heed to yourselves, lest at any time your hearts be overcharged with surfeiting, and drunkenness, and cares of this life, and so that day come upon you unawares. For as a snare shall it come on all them that dwell on the face of the whole earth"

(Luke 21:34-35). St. Paul said that believers are to use this world but not misuse it. It is the gradual misuse that poses the snare. The creeping involvement in cares, riches and pleasures of this world is a deadly threat to spiritual life and fruitfulness. Yet it is perfectly evident that just this creeping involvement is presently overtaking a multitude of professed Christians. It is time to take the warning of Jesus seriously and remain disentangled!

PRINCIPLE THREE: TOTAL VICTORY

Israel's offer of peace was rejected. Sihon and Og both brought out their armies and made war. But God gave His people total victory. The armies of the enemies were destroyed, and the land, which was large and fruitful, became the permanent possession of Israel. They were "more than conquerors" through the power of God, for they not only won the battle; they became much richer in the process.

My friend, God wants His Church to be in constant victory also. After listing the many forces that are arrayed against us, St. Paul exulted, "In all these things we are more than conquerors through him that loved us" (Rom. 8:37).

PRINCIPLE FOUR: DELIVERANCE FOR THE CAPTIVES

We have seen this illustrated in the last two battles we have studied, and here it is again. Sihon of the Amorites was a warrior. He had attacked Moab to the south and had taken much of its land and people for himself. In Israel's song of victory she told the story: "Woe to thee, Moab! . . . he hath given his sons that escaped, and his daughters, into captivity unto Sihon king of the Amorites. We have shot at them . . . we have laid them waste" (Num. 21:29-30). Israel had compassion on these captive peoples and set them at liberty.

Let me repeat it: this is our purpose toward the world, to bring its people out from sins's captivity, not to be ensnared by it.

PRINCIPLE FIVE: BE NOT CONFORMED TO THIS WORLD

After winning climactic victories over Sihon and Og, Israel fell prey to the seductions of Balak. It is a sad story, but one that is mentioned often in the New Testament as a warning for the Church in the last days. Balak hired Balaam the prophet to come and curse Israel. God would not permit this, and Balak was infuriated over his failure. As a means of collecting his reward, however, Balaam proposed that Moab seduce Israel into religious cooperation, which involved idolatry and fornication as an act of idol worship. And Israel was taken in by the seduction, to their own disastrous loss. Indeed, 24,000 people died in the plague that followed!

St. Paul refers to this incident in I Corinthians 10, where he warns, "Now these things were our examples, to the intent we should not lust after evil things, as they also lusted" (v. 6). The last three writers of the New Testament, Peter, Jude, and John also use this story as a warning. The final reference is in Jesus' message to the Church at Pergamos, Revelation 2:14, "I have a few things against thee, because thou hast there them that hold the doctrine of Balaam, who taught Balak to cast a stumblingblock before the children of Israel, to eat things sacrificed unto idols, and to commit fornication."

Can you believe such a thing, that the church would make a doctrine out of Balaam's plot to seduce Israel? It is the doctrine of conformity—the teaching that we can be more effective in winning the world if we are more like the world. This doctrine is extremely popular today. Young people are being taught that they do not need to give up the pleasures of the world to be Christians. They can share the same goals, follow the same fashions, listen to the same forms of music, act very much at home here in this world, and still be fine Christians. We hear talk now about Christian rock stars, Christian homosexuals, Christian alcoholics, and much more. It is time to remember the command of St. Paul, "Be not conformed to this world: but be ye transformed by the renewing of your mind, that ye may prove what is that good, and acceptable, and perfect, will of God" (Rom. 12:2). That suggests what is certainly true: *a person will never know the delights of God's perfect will while endeavoring to fit into the world's mold.*

The Church, by its very name, is a "called out" body. Her citizenship is in another country. If she is not willing to be different, it is because she really IS NOT; she is not transformed yet. She may bear the name of the church, but she is still a part of the world. God's true Church is separated from the world and happy to be so. She does not pine away for the world's pleasures, for she has richer delights to enjoy. She is not running breathlessly after some new fashion or fad; her heart is at rest in the Lord, and she delights in her Master's will.

To summarize this lesson: the Church is not to settle down and be at home in this world. We are pilgrims here and are not ashamed of the identification. At the same time we have a mission to fulfill. We are on a "search and recovery" operation. It is fine to make friends with those who are lost in this world, if we do not compromise our principles in doing so. When we keep our principles clear and follow the king's highway, we can have the same assurance God gave Moses concerning the giant king Og, "Fear him not: for I have delivered him into thy hand" (Num. 21:34).

It is God's battle, you see, and He always gives the victory to His people!

8

GOD'S GIFT OF JERICHO

We come now to one of the most interesting stories of conquest in all the Bible, and I am calling it, "God's Gift of Jericho." It is found in Joshua, chapter 6. In v. 16, "Joshua said unto the people, Shout; for the Lord hath given you the city."

That has to be one of the strangest gifts God ever gave. Jericho was the gateway to all of Canaan, the best fortified city in the land. It had fine houses, markets, supplies of food and livestock, all of which would be attractive to a people who had wandered for 40 years and who were surely ready to settle down for a while.

But God's command, however, was that every living thing in the city should be slain; everything that could be burnt was to be destroyed by fire, and every treasure that wouldn't burn—jewels, gold and silver—was to be brought into the treasury of God's house. Moreover, any man who would dare to rebuild the city would be under a curse.

And this was God's gift to His people! A heap of ashes and rubble! Is that the way God gives to His children? Sometimes it does appear so, and if we don't understand the significance of this event, we may find ourselves among those who think that God even today is eager to "rip people off," keeping back from them every good thing and leaving them nothing but the ashes of burnt-out hopes and dreams.

What does this gift of Jericho represent? It is so important that we understand this. As we have seen before, the Holy Land represents the holy life, the life of spiritual rest in the victory of Christ. And this first conquest in Canaan represents the infilling with the Holy Spirit at the beginning of such a life. Let me establish that fact.

First, the Hebrew word for "Jericho" is very similar to the word for "spirit." There is apparently a close kinship between the two.

Second, as the captain of the Lord's host instructed Joshua how to take the city, so the Lord Jesus told His disciples how to receive the Spirit. They were to "tarry in the city of Jerusalem, until [they were] endued with power from on high" (Luke 24:49).

Third, the time of waiting was the same in each case: seven days. When these facts are added together, the spiritual principle involved here seems clear. But it will become even more evident as we proceed.

The host of Israel had to pass four tests in order to take Jericho, and the child of God must pass the same four tests to be filled with God's Holy Spirit. I do not mean that the Spirit is given as a reward for labor, any more than Jericho was earned by 13 trips of marching around the city. But there were conditions to be met then, and there are now, also, for those who desire God's fulness.

TEST #1

First was the *test of destruction.* Every fleshly thing had to be slain. Verse 21 records it: "And they utterly destroyed all that was in the city, both man and woman, young and old, and ox, and sheep, and ass, with the edge of the sword." That may appear extremely severe, until we understand the condition which prevailed there. God had not brought His people into the land of Canaan until He saw that the residents there were saturated with sin and ripe for destruction. Those people were worshipers of Venus, and they regularly combined fornication with Venus worship. Social diseases were rampant among them. In fact, the word "venereal" comes from the name "Venus," with which the diseases were thus connected. God did not want His people infected with such loathesome and deadly plagues, so the land was to be totally purged of sinful flesh.

There is a destruction that must occur in the believer also. There must be a total end to the principle of fleshly living. St. Paul wrote to the believers at Rome, saying, "Knowing this, that our old man is crucified with him, that the body of sin might be destroyed, that henceforth we should not serve sin" (Rom. 6:6). You see, the body of sin must be destroyed, abruptly and finally.What is this body of sin? First, look at another statement from the Apostle, in Galatians 5:24, "And they that are Christ's have crucified the flesh with its affections and lusts." What is this "flesh" that is crucified? The two are closely related. The "body of sin" refers not to the human body itself but to the principle of sin that dwells within the body and operates through it. The "flesh" refers to the whole of life lived under the influence of sin. In Galatians 5:19-21, works of the flesh are listed. Some of them are matters of bodily conduct, such as adultery, but several others are inner attitudes of the mind, such as hatred, wrath, and envyings. They are still said to be of the flesh, because the flesh here does not mean the body, but sin residing within the body and expressing itself in a great many ways.

There must be a time of destruction when those attitudes such as hatred, wrath, envy, pride, and many more, are radically purged by the blood of Jesus Christ. According to I John 1:7 that purging is promised to those who walk in God's light: "If we walk in the light, as he is in the light, we have fellowship one with another; and the blood of Jesus Christ His Son cleanseth us from all sin."

TEST #2

Second was the *test of consecration.* Verse 19 gives us the command: "But all the silver, and gold, and vessels of brass and iron, are consecrated unto the Lord: they shall come into the treasury of the Lord." When a person is converted, every EVIL thing is renounced. There is not any real repentance if that is not so. But now there is a stricter test: every GOOD thing is given up to God. It is easy to see why the evil must be renounced, but why the good? Does God not want us to enjoy the good things? Is He just a big kill-joy who delights in taking things away from people?

It is highly important that we get this matter straight, for there is a dangerous doctrine growing today which says that God really DOES want us to have what we like, and He would never take it away from us. Let us look at some examples to understand the truth. Jesus asked the rich young ruler to sell all his possessions, give the money to the poor and follow Him. But the man went away sorrowful because he loved those possessions more than he loved Jesus. Jesus did not cater, you see, to the young man's desires.

St. Paul said of his own consecration, in Philippians 3:7-8, "What things were gain to me, those I counted loss for Christ. Yea doubtless, and I count all things but loss for the excellency of the knowledge of Christ Jesus my Lord: for whom I have suffered the loss of all things, and do count them but dung, that I may win Christ." Note that he suffered the ordeal, watching all of his ambitions and assets go for nothing at all, until he had only empty hands left for the Lord to fill with Himself. That is a painful process for anybody! You cannot give up your dearest dreams, your most valued assets, your closest friendships, without suffering!

Observe one more scripture, Luke 14:33, in which Jesus generalizes this principle of total consecration: "Whosoever he be of you that forsaketh not all that he hath, he cannot be my disciple." And He specified what the "all things" included: father, mother, wife, children, brothers, sisters, and his own life as well. That means nothing at all can be held back.

But why is this? Why does God want to reduce us to nothing? Here's the reason. You see, by every right we do belong to God. He created us for Himself. Then when we sinned against Him, He redeemed us through the Calvary sacrifice of His own Son so we really do belong to Him and not to ourselves. But it is the devil's lie that we are gods in our own lives. That is what he persuaded Eve to believe in the Garden, and he has every new generation believing the same thing: "My life is my own, and I can do as I please with it."

If we are to have God's fulness in our lives we must begin with the fundamental fact that everything belongs to Him, not to us. God doesn't always take every possession from us literally, but the principle must be settled: He has a right to it all; it is not ours anymore! Jesus Christ is Lord of all!

Once this consecration is settled, we begin to enter the fulness of God's perfect will and to find the rich fulfilment that comes from it. After Israel obeyed God in consecrating Jericho's treasures to Him, He gave them riches from many other cities which they conquered. He never intended to leave them paupers but to enrich them with victories so long as they followed Him as Lord.

There was one man, though, who could not wait. He insisted on having his portion right there in Jericho. So he stole 200 shekels of silver, 50 shekels of gold, and a fancy Babylonish garment. But God saw the fraud and withheld His further blessings until it was fully confessed, and the traitor, Achan, was put to death.

You see, God is absolutely serious about this matter of total consecration. I hope you are too, my dear friend. If you are to know the fulness of God's Spirit, there can be no compromise here at all. By yielding your all, painful as it may seem at the moment, you are preparing for God's fulness, which is far, far better.

TEST #3

God commanded that the people march around Jericho once a day for six days, then seven times around on the seventh day—thirteen trips in all. As if that were not enough of a *test of obedience*, then listen to this: "And Joshua had commanded the people saying, Ye shall not shout, nor make any noise with your voice, neither shall any word proceed out of your mouth, until the day I bid you shout; then shall ye shout"(v. 10). Can you imagine it? The whole host of Israel marching day after day, and not a word ever spoken! I can just imagine some of the ladies bringing up the rear beginning to say, "Wow, my feet are killing me! I don't feel like going a step farther." But the order was, "Quiet! No complaints allowed." They were learning to obey whether they felt like it or not.

That's exactly our test of obedience, too. Do we obey God just when we feel like it, or do we obey at all times and at all costs? If Jesus is Lord, we obey Him regardless of feelings.

Now I hear some of the fellows whispering, "What's the reason for all this? I don't mind walking if I'm going somewhere. But this going in circles doesn't make any sense. I've got to have good reasons for what I'm doing. After all, I do have a bit of intelligence!"

"Quiet, fellows! This isn't a test of your intelligence but of your obedience. God is in charge of this operation, and His wisdom, not yours, is in control. Will you obey Him even when you can't understand, just because He is Lord of all?"

Oh, now somebody else is trying to talk. "I just can't take this mockery! The guards on the wall are laughing us to scorn. Look up there. They think we're a bunch of idiots, walking round and round like so many robots, saying nothing, accomplishing nothing. And I think it is stupid, to go on like this!"

Well, I think you get the point. Some are afraid, thinking all the enemy forces in the land will gather against them while they waste these precious days. Others are unbelievers—just sure this is wasted time and nothing will come from it. But God is putting them to a real test. Will they just go on marching, and let their doubts, their fears, their feelings die, because they are obeying God, and He knows what He is doing?

We all have wills of our own, and it is not easy to yield them totally to the will of God when we do not understand where He is leading us. But remember, He is Lord, infinite in wisdom, majestic in strength, and worthy of our unqualified obedience. We can obey when we do not understand, because He *does* understand. He is following out His own battle plan, not ours! That is so good to know! And it is so good to trust and follow where He leads! For He always wins His battles if His people will just obey His orders!

Are you prepared for this kind of obedience, neighbor? Or are you still putting your will above God's will? Remember, "The Holy Ghost . . . [is] given to them that obey Him" (Acts 5:32), and you will just never have the Gift if you are not ready to obey, without question and without complaint.

Even Jesus met this condition of obedience when He came as a man to earth. Here is how the writer put it in Hebrews 5:8-9, "Though he were a Son, yet learned he obedience by the things which he suffered; and being made perfect, he became the author of eternal salvation unto all them that obey him." Yes, He had a supremely wise and infinitely powerful will of His own. He could have mustered armies, conquered kingdoms, and become king of the nations. But when on earth, He put that all aside to obey His Father, even unto death. He said, "I do nothing of myself . . . he that sent me is with me: the Father hath not left me alone; for I do always those things that please him" (John 8:28-29).

Because of His willing submission, "God also hath highly exalted him, and given him a name which is above every name:

that at the name of Jesus every knee should bow . . . and that every tongue should confess that Jesus Christ is Lord, to the glory of God the Father" (Phil. 2:9-11).

You, too, can know an eternal fulfillment that comes through surrender to His Lordship, and obedience to His will!

TEST #4

Finally there is the *test of faith.* Joshua commanded the people, "Shout; for the Lord hath given you the city." Again I seem to hear some doubters talking: "What do you mean, He hath given us the city? The walls are still standing just like they were on Day One. The guards are still laughing down at us, and they are still in possession of the city. We're still outside, and we haven't gained a thing by all this walking. Let the walls fall down, and then I'll shout. But I won't shout until they do!" Yes, Sir, that is the language of doubt and fear: "I've got to see or feel before I believe." But in God's pattern we must believe in order to see. They were to shout first, and then the walls would fall down. That is the shout of faith.

We must understand that faith is inseparably related to obedience. They were not to shout until they had circled the city wall thirteen times. But now they had done so; there were no more journeys to make, no more conditions to meet—except to shout for victory.

Joshua said, "The Lord hath given you the city" (past tense.) "It's already yours, so shout about it." Let me ask you: had God really given them the city already? Was it actually theirs, even before they entered it? Absolutely! God had already transferred title to them, and it was theirs by right of ownership because they had fully obeyed His conditions for taking it. Because they had obeyed His Word they could trust His Word and claim what He said was theirs.

So they shouted with a great shout, and sure enough! the walls came crashing down. They entered and took possession of what was theirs.

Claiming God's fulness through the Holy Spirit follows the same pattern. We must pass the *tests of death* to the fleshly principle of sins; *of consecration,* until every possession and every ambition is presented to Him; *of obedience,* until we are ready to do His will with no reservations; *then of faith,* claiming what is ours on the basis of His promise alone. The sinful heart is an unbelieving heart, though, and generally there will be a whisper from within, "You don't dare to believe God; nothing's going to happen. You don't feel any victory. You've got to have some big sensation first, some big show of power." Well, that whisper is the spirit of unbelief, and it has to die with all the other sinful attitudes that have brought defeat and failure.

Israel may not have felt like shouting, but they shouted anyway and victory came.

There was once a weak-minded boy name Tommy who was out in a field by himself, shouting aloud. Some other boys passed by and asked, "Tommy, what in the world are you doing?"

"I'm shouting for joy," he said. "The joy hasn't come yet, but I'm shouting for it anyway."

Now that is the attitude of real faith, such certainty about what is coming that we count it as good as done.

In Romans 6:11, St. Paul said, "Likewise reckon yourselves to be dead indeed unto sin, but alive unto God through Jesus Christ our Lord." That word "reckon" is a bookkeeping word, but it is also a faith word. It means to enter something in your books and count it as a fact.

I went into the Air Force before Pearl Harbor, and because of that the U. S. Government promised a bonus of $500 for each year of commissioned service, though I was not aware of that fact when I enlisted. Sure enough, after my release from active duty there came a check from the U.S. Treasury for $2100. I had never seen such a check before, much less owned one! But I took it to the bank where I had opened a small account and showed it to the cashier. She was amazed at the size of it, but she wrote the amount in my receipt book, adding it to my account. And I entered the same figure in my checkbook. You see, I was reckoning something as mine that I had not seen. I hadn't seen the money, but I started acting like it was mine. And every check I drew on that amount was good—as good as the U.S. Treasury.

There comes a time when we have passed all the tests. The Holy Spirit is ours, because God has promised Him to us who believe. He may demonstrate His presence in many ways, but His presence is not there due to the demonstration. He is there, and He abides, because we follow Jesus as Lord, and walk on with Him by faith.

9

LEARNING
FROM FAILURE

Have you learned that some of our greatest victories today are recoveries from the defeats of yesterday? The Bible battle in this study is an example. It is the story of Ai, found in Joshua, chapters 7 and 8.

After the colossal victory at Jericho, some spies were sent to Ai, about ten miles to the west, to evaluate the best course of battle there. They reported only a little city and recommended that only a small force of some 3,000 men go up to subdue it.

The engagement turned into a rout, and Israel was badly defeated. Only 36 men died, but the sense of failure was devastating. Joshua fell on his face before God and complained bitterly of the defeat. It would have been better, he said, if Israel had never come into Canaan at all. Now the enemies of the Lord would find that His people were highly vulnerable after all. And what would the Lord God do about His reputation?

That is the background story, and we want to see what lessons there are in it for us today—for the Church in her spiritual warfare.

WHOSE FAULT IS FAILURE?

Here is the *first lesson,* and it is an important one: *Don't blame God for your failures!* Joshua, with the elders of Israel, had been prostrated on the ground before the Lord, with clothes rent and dust on their heads. Finally at evening time the Lord spoke and said, "Get thee up; wherefore liest thou thus upon they face? Israel hath sinned, and they have also transgressed my covenant which I commanded them" (vs. 10-11).

You see, Joshua did not know what had gone on behind the scenes, but the Lord did. He saw the secret sin that had occurred at Jericho, and this failure came as a consequence. To Joshua it looked like God had simply failed His people in a most miserable way, and He held God accountable for it. The Lord needed to shape up and do a better job of overcoming the enemy! That was Joshua's assessment.

How easy it is to come to such a conclusion! There is so much we have to learn about spiritual conflict and the forces involved! Because we cannot see the spiritual forces, it is easy to conclude they are not there, and God has simply failed to come through with victory.

Do you remember the story of Job? It is a classic account of spiritual forces working against the great saint—forces which he could not see. So he concluded God was responsible for his troubles, and he made some serious charges about God's wisdom. When God answered, He demonstrated it was Job who did not know what was going on, and Job did not know enough criticize the Lord! That is a lesson we all need to learn, and the sooner the better. We do not know enough to criticize the Lord! Wait patiently for the Lord to answer, and you will find He never fails, not for one instant! He is never caught off guard, never too slow, and never forgetful.

Ask God to help you learn your lessons and profit from your mistakes. He is a wonderful Teacher, and He will help you recover from your failures.

THE HANDICAP OF HIDDEN SIN

Here is the *second lesson: Do not expect victory over covered sin!* A man named Achan had sinned at Jericho. He felt the covenant of consecration there was too strict. God, you recall, had asked that every piece of money—gold and silver—be brought into the treasury of the Lord. Achan did not like that. He felt he had earned the right to enjoy some of the loot. Others could be that strict if they liked, but he would be more practical. So he took five pounds of silver, a pound and a quarter of gold, and a beautiful robe from Babylon, and hid them all in his tent. Nobody would know, he thought.

Is it not easy for people to reason that way? "Nobody will know. Nobody saw me do it. I'll just keep it under cover for a while, and outsmart everybody!" What foolish thinking that is! It is strictly carnal thinking—earthly thinking—and it overlooks the most important fact of all: God sees it, and He takes it all into account. How we need to learn the lesson that God sees it all, and while we may seem to get by for a while, there is an accounting ahead! There is a reckoning day coming!

And what a reckoning it was for Achan! He had to make confession and restitution. And then the people of Israel stoned him with stones for his sinful folly!

A young lady in my church fell into the wrong company. Her folks would not know, she thought. She would play with temptation for just a little while. But then she was caught in the trap of lust! She ran away from home to be with relatives 1,000 miles away. But soon she was back and visited me in my home. "Oh, I couldn't get away from my conscience," she cried. Her sin was with her, and so was an unwanted child, soon to be born. How bitter the consequences of that foolish notion, "Nobody will know!" Well, God knows, and you know, and you cannot have any real peace until you come clean and make full confession!

Here is a surprising part of the story of Achan. God held the whole nation of Israel accountable for his sin until it was confessed and discipline administered. Of course God knew from the first who committed that sin, but He did not say. He asked the whole nation to appear before Him for inspection. There He chose the tribe of Judah, then the family of Zerah, next the household of Zabdi, and finally the man, Achan.

Maybe you think that is just an Old Testament story, and it means nothing for us today. Then look in Revelation 2:12-16, at Christ's message to the Church at Pergamos. He commended them highly, saying, "Thou holdest fast my name, and hast not denied my faith." But then He revealed something wrong: "Thou hast there them that hold the doctrine of Balaam . . . So hast thou also them that hold the doctrine of the Nicolaitans, which thing I hate." Both of these were doctrines of compromise with the world, and God hates them! So here is what Jesus said (v. 16), "Repent; or else I will come unto thee quickly, and will fight against them with the sword of my mouth." Here are faithful people, commended for their integrity; yet Jesus called them all to repentance because of the false teachers hidden away there in the church!

You see, the Church is not just so many individuals; it is a body—Christ's body. And whatever affects one affects all. Sin covered by one little part of the body may seem to escape notice. But God sees it, and He will not give that Church the victory He wants it to have until the sin is removed. Oh, we can have a human program going on with a fair show of success, but it will never be God's kind of victory until there is a purging and the sin is removed.

The Church must live so close to God that He can reveal her true state at any time, as He sees her. The Church must be so effective in prayer, and so united in purpose, that covered sin just does not stay there spreading its poison but is revealed in God's light and brought to an end. That is God's way of victory for His Church!

TOTAL VICTORY TAKES TOTAL INVOLVEMENT

Let me give you one final lesson from the story of Ai: *total victory requires total involvement!* The spies said only a small army was needed to fight that battle. After their defeat God spoke and said to Joshua, "Take all the people of war with thee, and arise, go up to Ai." You see, God was not satisfied with little token forces. The whole army was involved, and He wanted them to act like it. So they all went to Ai, and God gave them total victory. This time, though, they were permitted to keep all the wealth of the city for themselves. They were enriched abundantly by their victory!

This is a lesson for the Church also. The Spirit of God will never approve part-time devotion, half-hearted loyalty, or lukewarm service for Christ or His Church! If we are only half involved, then we are facing failure like Israel did at Ai.

In I Corinthians 12 St. Paul describes the Church as a body—the body of Christ. He makes it emphatic that every member has a gift, has a ministry to perform. Every member has some manifestation of the Spirit to use for the benefit of the whole body. Likewise, in Ephesians 4 he stresses that every member is called of God to share in the ministry of the body. In verse 16 he summarizes the results: "From [Christ the head] the whole body fitly joined together and compacted by that which every joint supplieth, according to the effectual working in the measure of every part, maketh increase of the body unto the edifying of itself in love" (v. 16). That means that if every member is functioning according to its ability, the body will increase outward and upward at the same time! It will grow both in size and in spiritual stature.

My friend, these are great lessons for us! How vital it is that we apply them! These Old Testament stories are not mere historical incidents. They are replete with truth for us today. I hope and pray we can appropriate them so the Church will be victorious in spiritual warfare.

10

STAR WARS

This study about "Star Wars," is taken from Judges 5:20, "They fought from heaven; the stars in their courses fought against Sisera." Let's look at a little of the background from Chapter 4, verses 1-7:

> *And the Children of Israel again did evil in the sight of the Lord, ... And the Lord sold them into the hand of Jabin King of Canaan, ... the captain of whose host was Sisera, ... and the children of Israel cried unto the Lord: for he had nine-hundred chariots of iron; and twenty years he mightily oppressed the children of Israel. And Deborah, a prophetess, ... she judged Israel at that time. ... And she sent and called Barak the son of Abinoam ... and said unto him, Hath not the Lord God of Israel commanded, saying, Go and draw toward mount Tabor, and take with thee ten-thousand men of the children of Naphtali and of the children of Zebulun? And I will draw unto thee to the river Kishon Sisera, the captain of Jabin's army, with his chariots and his multitude; and I will deliver him into thine hand.*

THE PREDICAMENT OF ISRAEL

In this fascinating chapter of Israel's history, there are three special features that stand out. The first is their *compromise*, then the *commitment* of some of them, and finally the *conquest* through which their miraculous deliverance came.

Israel's sad situation, I say, was a result of tragic COM-PROMISE. God had told them that if they allowed the pagan people of the land to remain undestroyed, those people would become as pricks in Israel's eyes and as thorns in their sides. Even worse, God Himself would turn and bring judgment upon them. In spite of the warnings, though, Israel left, here and there, little pockets of the enemy who were made into slaves instead of being put to death. At first this seemed such a reasonable thing to do. The pagans were so few as to pose no threat, and they could do a lot of work for God's people.

But years had passed and those people had multiplied in number and in strength. They had become organized with a king, and now had Israel in the place of slavery. Israel would plant, but the Canaanites would plunder the harvest. Survival became a desperate problem of working in secret, staying off the main roads, and hiding food supplies from the enemy.

Now this illustrates a most important lesson about our spiritual warfare: *we never win by compromise!* You may recall that those enemy tribes represent sinful traits in human hearts and lives. Sometimes it appears so reasonable to make little concessions to dishonesty, retaliation, or greed. Very possibly you are conscious of just such a compromise in your life. It seems so useful to cheat a little in your business or even in your marriage. Just a little will not hurt, you reason. But will you remember this lesson of Israel? Little compromises grow into big ones. Sin is never barren! It reproduces and multiplies, just like those Canaanites did, and finally it gets the upper hand. Then it brings misery, slavery and failure. My friend, we never win spiritual battles by compromise with evil!

Out of Israel's desperate condition they began to cry to God for help. That is always a good thing to do when we see our own failure and loss. In one of David's Psalms he said, "This poor man cried, and the Lord heard him, and saved him out of all his troubles." If you are in trouble today because of some concession to sin, you, too, can cry to God, and I assure you He is ready to hear you.

The second feature of the story is a lesson about COMMIT-MENT. Israel had been under oppression for 20 years, and they were almost totally unarmed. Two tribes out of twelve responded to the call for soldier volunteers, and out of these two—Zebulun and Naphtali—10,000 men were chosen to fight.

What a lopsided engagement that was! A multitude of armed men on one side with 900 chariots and horsemen, while on the other side were a mere 10,000 mostly unarmed men. But this was God's battle, you see. It was His honor that was at stake; His people were in bondage. He was moving in answer to prayer, and He always knows how to move when His people begin to pray in earnest!

The Lord God revealed to Deborah His strategy for victory, and she in turn relayed it to Barak, the commander of forces. God said those 10,000 men should go to the top of Mt. Tabor, and from there they should charge down into the face of the opposing army.

Tabor was about 15 miles west of the Sea of Galilee. Farther to the west, and flowing into the Mediterranean Sea, was the great river Kishon. Two of the tributaries formed a "V," with rather level plain between them. Tabor was near the upper center of that "V." The Canaanites under Sisera occupied the plain, and Barak's 10,000 men were on the mountain. At God's command those soldiers rushed down from the mountain in a frontal assault on the enemy. Now the name Barak means "Lightning," so I like to call this "The Charge of the Lightning Brigade."

What a beautiful example of commitment this was! Badly outnumbered, pitifully unequipped, and utterly hopeless from the natural standpoint, these men nevertheless committed themselves to God's battle without reservation! In her song of victory, Judges chapter 5, Deborah wrote, "Zebulun and Naphtali were a people that jeoparded their lives unto the death in the high places of the field!" Well, that is the faith that draws on God's mighty resources, gives everything to His cause, and watches Him win His battles!

There will be more about the matter of commitment later in the chapter, but here I want to talk about the CONQUEST which resulted. Josephus, the ancient Jewish historian, tells that right at the time when Barak's brigade charged down the mountainside, God sent a phenomenal storm of rain and hail, driven by a strong east wind. This came to the backs of Barak's men, but it blew full in the face of men and horses in the opposing army. The horses panicked and fled, turning upon their own men. Confused and blinded, the Canaanite soldiers attacked one another or ran in terror. Seizing the initiative, Barak's forces pursued until the enemy became mired in the flooded plain or actually ran into the Kishon river and drowned. Here is how Deborah put it in her song: "The river of Kishon swept them away, that ancient river, the river Kishon. O my soul, thou hast trodden down strength" (v. 21).

When Deborah spoke of the stars fighting against Sisera's armies, she evidently referred to God's use of natural forces to bring down a strong and proud foe. The rain, hail and wind from the heavens served to assist the little unarmed band but confounded the charioteers and multiplied ranks of foot soldiers. The plains, normally suited well to chariot maneuvers, became swamps of mud. The two tributaries of the Kishon, now uncrossable torrents, funneled the fleeing troops right into the great river, to their own destruction.

We could think of many other illustrations of how God uses the forces of heaven and earth to work His will. For example, there was the east wind which opened the Red Sea and let the army of Israel pass through on dry ground. Then when Egypt pursued after them into the Sea, the Lord "turned off" the wind and let the waters return and cover defiant Pharaoh and his armed forces.

It is a matter of record that in more recent times, when the Nazi forces were within hours of total victory over Britain in World War II, the tide of battle was miraculously turned, and the Nazis suffered a colossal defeat. In a Bible college in Wales, Rees Howells, the principal, and his staff, spent from 8 p.m. until midnight daily, praying for God to spare Britain and bring down the Nazi peril so the gospel could continue to be proclaimed freely from the Commonwealth. And at a time when the fleeing Allied Forces were trapped at Dunkirk, God sent a heavy fog over those weary troops and let them all escape safely across the Channel instead of being obliterated by their pursuers. To God be the glory; great things He hath done!

And my friends, there is coming another great day of battle, when it will appear that Antichrist's forces are destroying the last stronghold of Christian faith and gaining total victory for materialism, humanism and unbelief. But that is not the end! Jesus holds the powers of heaven and earth in His hands. Listen to the words of Revelation 6, verses 12-17, when the sixth seal of judgment is opened:

Lo, there was a great earthquake; and the sun became
black as sackcloth of hair, and the moon became as
blood; and the stars of heaven fell unto the earth, . . .
And the kings of the earth, and the great men, and the
rich men, and the chief captains, and the mighty men,
. . . hid themselves in the dens and in the rocks of the
mountains; and said to the mountains and rocks, Fall
on us, and hide us from the face of him that sitteth on
the throne, and from the wrath of the Lamb: for the great
day of his wrath is come; and who shall be able to stand?

Do not forget it, neighbor; the Christ Who seems as meek as a
lamb today, Who offers Himself to you as your Savior, is still
Governor of the universe. He is Judge of all the earth, and He
will win His fight against sin and all injustice.

PRINCIPLES OF VICTORY

Next I want us to examine the Principles of Victory. Here
is the first principle: *"Faith Triumphs Over Discouragement."*
There was plenty to be discouraged about in those days. The land
had been under enemy control for twenty years. The Canaanites
were so strong, and Israel was so weak, that for many the situation seemed utterly hopeless. There were no arms available for
fighting; the army was untrained and small. How could there be
any hope? Most folks just accepted the bondage as unchangeable.

Do you know that is one of our greatest dangers: to accept
a long-standing problem as insoluble and adjust ourselves to it
as inevitable? Look at some of the problems the church faces
today: drug addiction, pornography, divorce, abortion, humanism
in society, the unevangelized billions that make up half the world's
population—these and others that could be mentioned. Are we
attacking them in faith, or have we ceased to protest and accepted
them as unavoidable?

Well, in Israel things began to change, and it started with
one woman of faith named Deborah. Here is one verse in her victory song: "The inhabitants of the villages ceased, they ceased
in Israel until that I Deborah arose, that I arose a mother in
Israel." What a pungent phrase that is: a "mother in Israel!" A
mother travails until she brings forth. And Deborah travailed
before God for her nation, until He intervened and turned her travail into a new birth of freedom.

I tell you, we need more "mothers in Israel" today for our land, for our nation and for our churches—people who know how to travail in intercession until our God intervenes from Heaven in behalf of His people. Human action is necessary, but if there is no supernatural help from the God of battles, we will be swallowed up by our problems. Of course, we can just ignore them as inescapable elements of modern society, but "mothers in Israel" will not be so easily reconciled to defeat. Their faith will overcome their discouragement, and God will answer them!

God gave to Deborah a plan of victory, including the number and position of her forces. He assured her of the outcome as well. It all looked highly unreasonable: 10,000 mostly unarmed men going against the multitude of Sisera's forces, with their 900 chariots of iron. But Deborah believed God, and declared unto Barak, "Up, for this is the day in which the Lord hath delivered Sisera into thine hand: is not the Lord gone out before thee?" And Barak also responded in faith, leading His "Lightning Brigade" to brilliant victory.

It is this kind of fervent intercession, followed with unwavering faith, that opens up God's resources of victory. As St. John said, "This is the victory that overcometh the world, even your faith." So renounce your doubts today, pray with faith, and look for the God of battles to intervene in the conflict!

I do not know what part God has for you to do in this battle against the forces of evil, but it is an important part, because the assignment comes from Him. Do not be intimidated because nobody else sees what you see or believes what you believe. Deborah was very much alone, but God brought her to victory, and He will do the same for you! You can be an effective witness; you can pioneer a new church; you can be a successful missionary, if that is God's assignment for you. You can be a mother—or father—in Israel; you can make a difference, by God's help!

Here is the second principle of victory: "*Dedication Triumphs Over Distraction.*" Just as it is today, there were many things which served to distract some of the people from joining in the battle for deliverance. Deborah named the people in her song of praise and showed what their distractions were. There was first the distraction of **pleasure**. In Judges 5:16 Deborah named the tribe of Reuben and asked, "Why abodest thou among the sheepfolds, to hear the bleatings of the flocks? For the divisions of

Reuben there were great searchings of heart." Some scholars believe the word "bleatings" refers to a sort of shepherd's pipe with which they made music around the campfires at night. While the people of Reuben were troubled in their consciences, the attraction of those musical "afterglows" prevailed over their sense of duty. It would bring more pleasure to stay by the campfires and let somebody else go and fight. So they debated, discussed, reasoned and refuted, until the challenge had passed, and they had lost their opportunity to serve God and country. The appeal of pleasure canceled out the sense of duty.

That same appeal is so common today! A missionary of my acquaintance was invited to speak in a Sunday missionary service. From her burdened heart she poured forth a story of physical and spiritual destitution among the people where she worked, appealing that we who have so much should rally to their aid. When she had finished the pastor—of all people—responded by saying, "Well, folks, you can thank God if He doesn't call you to serve in areas like that." He was really saying, "You can be happier in the soft, pleasureful life, so be glad if God doesn't ask you to face hardship." One of America's biggest problems is that we are too much in love with pleasure! We like the soft music and the afterglow, but we don't like the discomfort of the battlefront. Too often we join the troops of Reuben and stay by the campfires while Barak's Brigade does the fighting.

Second, there was the distraction of **distance**. Verse 17 says, "Gilead abode beyond Jordan." This verse refers to the tribe of Gad which dwelled east of the Jordan, while the battle was miles away to the west. They were just too far away to feel the sense of need.

That reminds me of a preacher who advertised his availability for a pastorate with this condition: it must be within driving distance of his own home. Well, Christ's great commission does not have that kind of clause in it. The Church is commanded to go into all the world. It is easy to forget a need when it is 10,000 miles away, but we need to be reminded that the hurting multitude is suffering just as much as if we witnessed every quiver of hurt at close range. Distance does not stop the pain, and it does not lessen our responsibility either!

Third, there was the distraction of **business**. In verse 17 Deborah asked, "Why did Dan remain in ships?" The answer is: because that was his business—his source of income and profit.

His business just might suffer loss if he left it and went to war for his nation. What if his country were at stake? What if the business might soon be lost to the enemy anyway? Those considerations were put out of mind. It was the immediate present that counted with Dan. The money in hand counted far more than future loss. He must be a hard-headed realist to succeed in the business. There was no time for idealism about the future welfare of a nation or even his own children. "Business is business," he said, and stayed with his ships, while a nation hung in the balance.

Fourth, was the distraction of **security**. "Asher continued on the seashore, and abode in his harbors," verse 17 continues. There in the safety of the harbor and the seashore he stayed until the danger had passed. It would be risking too much to go into enemy territory with such a small military force, especially one called to arms by a lady. No, it was safer to stay at home and let somebody else go to battle.

My friend, there are many people who are suffering from these same distractions today: pleasure, distance, business and security. They are mildly aware of a battle going on, but they are not involved. A serious student spoke to me one day after a college Bible class and said, "Our young people are not really interested in heavenly and eternal realities; they are too much involved in material things of the here and now." How about YOU, neighbor? Are you really in this fight against evil, against ignorance and unconcern? Or are you among the distracted?

However, there is a dedication that triumphs over distraction. Hear these words from Deborah's song: "My heart is toward the governors of Israel, that offered themselves willingly among the people. Bless ye the Lord. . . . Zebulun and Naphtali were a people that jeoparded their lives unto the death in the high places of the field." With that little band of dedicated people God won a mighty victory and saved a nation. The distracted people drew rebuke and shame. They missed the hour of heroism for a noble cause. Their names will live forever as examples of failure, while others were heroes of faith and dedication. How will yours and mine be remembered?

I worked for some years with a dear widow who spent her last 25 years in a small dormitory room, cooking on an electric hotplate and wearing made-over clothes. She taught in a Bible college and gave thousands of dollars to help young people prepare for the ministry. I visited her in the hospital during her last days. She said, "I'm sorry I've done so little for Jesus. I don't know how I can stand before Him, when He has done so much for me." But then she continued, "I guess when I see Him I'll just have to show Him my hands." Those hands were gnarled and disfigured by hard labors as well as disease. She had poured her very life into service for Jesus. She was not claiming the merit of works but was concerned as to whether she had done her best in serving Christ.

Well, I am concerned about the same thing, and I hope you are too. This is God's battle, and He is going to win it. There is no doubt about that! But what will your place and mine be in the victory celebration? It depends on our commitment to Christ and His cause.

11

STRATEGY
FOR SUCCESS

There had never been such a scandal since Israel left Egypt!
A Levite with his concubine stopped at Gibeah of Benjamin for
the night, and the men of the city so abused the woman that she
was found dead in the morning. The entire nation of Israel was
so indignant at this injustice toward a visitor that they summoned
an army of 400,000 men out of the remaining tribes to make war
against Benjamin.

INEFFECTIVE ASSETS

There were several indications that success was certain in the
battle, and they have their counterpart in missionary endeavors.
First, there was *strong commitment*, "All the people arose as one
man, saying, We will not any of us go to his tent, neither will
we any of us turn into his house" (Judges 20:8). In addition to
400,000 armed men, they volunteered ten per cent of their people
for support activities so justice might be accomplished against
the offending tribe. Such enthusiastic devotion to a cause is indeed
commendable. They were pledged to the cause of retribution. How
much more should every believer today be committed to the cause
of redemption through Jesus Christ!

Second, there was *unity*. "So all the men of Israel were
gathered against the city [Gibeah], knit together as one man"

(v. 11). What a fine figure that is! Men from eleven tribes worked together as efficiently as the members of one body. That is just the way St. Paul describes the Church when it is working effectively in both edification and enlargement (Eph. 4:16). No antagonisms or jealousies weakened the operation. No quarrel about leadership cast its shadow over it. Unity, efficiency and commitment were in fine form. There was bright hope of success.

Third, there was *adequate manpower.* Benjamin had only 26,000 men, while the other allied tribes had 400,000. Not a chance of failure appeared!

Finally, *they prayed and gained God's direction.* The army went to God's house and asked who should lead the way into battle. He responded that Judah should go first.

What fine prospects for victory! Organization, unity, strength, commitment; certainly this was an invincible alliance that must surely win!

But they did not. They lost terribly. Twenty-two thousand men were slain on that first day of battle. Yet Israel did not run away discouraged. "The men of Israel encouraged themselves, and set their battle again in array in the place where they put themselves in array the first day" (v. 22). Those people were not quitters. They knew how to encourage themselves when the situation was discouraging. They determined to go again before God, seeking fresh guidance. After a day of weeping and praying, they got God's directive to fight again. Surely the second day would bring victory!

But it did not! They lost 18,000 more men. Ten per cent of their total were gone in two days of failure. What should they do? How could they fail with such marked advantages? Why had God sent them into battle to be defeated?

SUCCESSFUL STRATEGY

The secret was a strategy. They were plainly using the wrong method. You see, Benjamin had a secret weapon! And Benjamin was victorious. Out-numbered more than 15 to one, that little tribe was still winning overwhelmingly. No wonder they had not been willing to negotiate! Do you know what that secret weapon was?

Benjamin had 700 left-handed sling-shooters, and "everyone could sling stones at an hair breadth, and not miss" (v. 16). The flying stones proved much more deadly than flaying swords. Before the men of Israel could get close enough to thrust in a sword, they were being neutralized by the deadly accuracy of 700 stone-throwers. Obviously there had to be a better strategy than the one which had brought them two days of costly defeat.

On the third day they fasted all day in prayer, offering burnt sacrifices and seeking fresh guidance from on high. God told them to go again and gain the victory. But before they went the third time, they introduced a new strategy, one that would nullify that deadly weapon of Benjamin. They planned an attack from ambush behind the city, while the main army, as before, approached in front of Gibeah. This time they won a colossal victory, destroying over 60 percent of the enemy forces with the loss of only 30 men of their own.

This story provides us a vital lesson in planning for effective missionary work. E. M. Bounds (Preacher and Prayer) is well known for his statement, "The world is looking for better methods; God is looking for better men." That has often been true. But it is an evident fact that sometimes the best of men need to find better methods. They need, like Israel, a strategy that will succeed. And like Israel, God lets them struggle along with their ineffective methods, losing valuable assets, until they put their intelligence to work and find that strategy. Doubtless, they were destroying a few of the Benjamites each day, and they might have been satisfied that this was victory. But they were forced to recognize that they would all be dead before the battle was over unless they found a better strategy. So they sought and found it, and they won.

Do we recognize that with all of our missionary efforts, this whole generation will be dead—yes, and more generations yet to come—before we win for the cause of missions, unless we find some better strategies?

Specifically, *we must find better means of challenging our young people with the urgency of missionary involvement.* They are being progressively secularized in today's society, and we are not effectively counteracting the deadly process. Moreover, *we must tap more resources of financial support,* for many of our efforts are limping along with inadequate funding. Again, *there must be strategy to enter new fields,* including the vast metropolitan areas of this and other countries. We are not reaching the great population centers of the world with our message, and in many instances we are not even making a creditable effort. Our excuse is that we are busy, and we don't have men or money for further outreach. And those excuses are real: we **are** busy, and we **are** short of men and money.

But Christ's command is that all the world **must** be reached before He comes again. We **must** find strategies that will help us complete that assignment. The best of men will keep on failing unless they find better strategies. Let us pray, weep, fast, and offer our sacrifices unto God, until He speaks His will. But let us use our intelligence also, until we discover methods that will win God's battle today. We can count on Him; can He count on us?

12

IS THERE NOT
A CAUSE?

Our next account of God's army comes from I Samuel chapter 17, from a story that we have all heard, enjoyed, and told to our children who have told it to their dolls—the story of David and Goliath. Beginning with verse 22, it reads,

> *And David left his carriage in the hand of the keeper of the carriage, and ran into the army, and came and saluted his brethren. And as he talked with them, behold, there came up the champion, the Philistine of Gath, Goliath by name, out of the armies of the Philistines, and spake according to the same words: and David heard them. And all the men of Israel, when they saw the man, fled from him, and were sore afraid. And the men in Israel said, Have ye seen this man that is come up? surely to defy Israel is he come up: . . . And David spake to the men that stood by him, saying, What shall be done to the man that killeth this Philistine, and taketh away the reproach from Israel? for who is this uncircumcised Philistine, that he should defy the armies of the living God? . . . And Eliab his eldest brother heard when he spake unto the men; and Eliab's anger was kindled against David, and he said, Why camest thou down hither? and with whom hast thou left*

*those few sheep in the wilderness? I know thy pride,
and the naughtiness of thine heart; for thou art come
down that thou mightest see the battle. And David said,
What have I now done? Is there not a cause? . . . And
the Philistine said to David, Come to me, and I will give
thy flesh unto the fowls of the air, and to the beasts of
the field. Then said David to the Philistine, Thou comest
to me with a sword, and with a spear, and with a shield:
but I come to thee in the name of the Lord of hosts,
the God of the armies of Israel, whom thou hast defied.
This day will the Lord deliver thee into mine hand; and
I will smite thee, and take thine head from thee; and
I will give the carcases of the host of the Philistines this
day unto the fowls of the air, and to the wild beasts of
the earth; that all the earth may know that there is a
God in Israel. And all this assembly shall know that
the Lord saveth not with sword and spear: for the battle is the Lord's, and he will give you into our hands.
And it came to pass, when the Philistine arose, and
came and drew nigh to meet David, that David hasted,
and ran toward the army to meet the Philistine. And
David put his hand in his bag, and took thence a stone,
and slang it, and smote the Philistine in his forehead,
that the stone sunk into his forehead; and he fell upon
his face to the earth.*

The text for our consideration is one of the questions David asked
in verse 29, "Is there not a cause?"

David did some unconventional things—things that those
near to him rejected and criticized—and he did them because there
was a cause—a cause worthy of that kind of commitment. The
cause is specified for us in verses 46 and 47 as he had it in his
heart and in his mind: "that ALL the earth may know that there
is a God in Israel. And all this assembly shall know that the Lord
saveth not with sword and spear: for the battle is the Lord's, and
he will give you into our hands." Israel was raised up for this very
purpose—to make all the earth know that there was a God in
Israel. They failed of that purpose miserably, and that purpose
has been committed now to the church—that all the earth may
know that there is a God.

David wanted the whole world to know something, but he also wanted the assembly to know something. The word "assembly" is one of the Old Testament forerunners of the New Testament word "church." Today God wants the world outside to know something, and He wants the church within to know something. He wants all the earth to know that God is alive, and that He is able to meet the challenges of today. He wants the church to know that the battle is His. When we commit ourselves to this high cause, the battle is God's battle and He will give us the victory if we keep our priorities straight. So this lesson of David and Goliath is actually a missionary story. Perhaps you have never thought of it as one before, but it is. David fought Goliath for a cause—that all the earth and all the assembly might know that God is able to fight our battles to victory.

THE GIGANTIC CHALLENGE

There was a gigantic challenge here, in the form of a flesh-and-blood giant. As I measure it, he was 9 feet 4 inches tall. Now that is a pretty good sized man! I have never seen anybody that big, that I can recall. He was a mighty challenge before the people of Israel. There is a gigantic challenge before us today, as the church. Our tremendous challenge is still there—it has not disappeared. In fact, this giant is getting bigger every day. It is the part of the world that is not yet reached with the gospel of Jesus Christ.

There are many ways we can describe this giant. One way is to say that when Jesus was here and was moved with compassion on the multitudes that were as sheep, fainting and without a shepherd, there were only 1/200th as many lost people in the world as there are now. Or, to put it in reverse, there are at least 200 times as many unevangelized people alive today as there were when Jesus was so greatly moved by the sight of those multitudes that needed to be reached. Another way we can express it is to say that today, according to the latest statistics I have, there are 16,000 unreached people groups in the world—unreached with the Gospel. Some of these are tribes, some of them are whole nations, and some of them are just small cultures within a larger culture, including some right here in our own United States, for example, immigrants from foreign countries who come here and settle in certain areas, and are not penetrated with the Gospel. 16,000 groups of people that are not yet reached with the

Gospel! Or picture our giant this way. If you were to line up the unevangelized of this earth in columns of four abreast and start them marching to military music past our point of observation, how long do you imagine it would take this column of unevangelized people to march past our observation post? They would never cease to march past—never! The number of unevangelized people being born is increasing so rapidly that by the time the present number marched past, they would be duplicated (and more) by others to follow by in their march. And unless the church of Jesus Christ does something better than they are now doing about penetrating these unreached multitudes, whether you and I see them marching by or not, they are marching—they are marching on to eternity without the message of the Gospel of Christ. That's a bigger challenge than Goliath. That is a mighty, gigantic challenge. I believe the gospel of full salvation. These examples do not include reaching people with the message of holiness. They simply refer to reaching them with the basics about getting saved—who Jesus is, and that there is a way to be saved from sin. The problem is even more mammoth when we talk about penetrating the world with the message of full salvation, and I believe that is our obligation. I believe that any who know this wonderful message of full deliverance from all sin have a serious and sacred obligation to share it with other people. I thank God for everybody who is preaching the Gospel that will get people saved from their sins, I really do! I thank God for all who are reaching people and are bringing them into the elementary truths of confession of sin and belief in the Lord Jesus Christ. But that does not dismiss our obligation to get out with the message of *full salvation.* That is an obligation—a gigantic, a truly monumental task that is before us. Is there not a cause? Indeed there is, a mighty and serious cause.

THE GROPING CHURCH

In the face of this gigantic challenge, look at the groping church, or the assembly, as it is called, not knowing what to do about the situation. It is almost comical to look back upon this scene. Verse 16 says "the Philistine drew near morning and evening, and presented himself forty days" to the army of Israel. Verse 20 says David came into the camp "as the host was going forth to the fight, and shouted for the battle." Can't you visualize the army of Israel shining their buckles, shining their boots, getting their armor all in array, all polished, all gleaming in the sun?! Their esprit de corps: they whip it up every morning and give a shout to go out to battle. What are they shouting about? Why, they're generating enthusiasm for the fight! They go out with a mighty shout! But when they get out—oh! there is that giant! They stop shouting, they turn around and march back into camp. Their esprit de corps is all gone, and their morale is descended to almost zero. The next morning they shine their shoes and they shine their buckles and they get their caps at exactly the right angle. Can't you see them? The band is playing, and they are marching—left, right, left, right—it is a beautiful sight! There they go! But oh! There's Goliath! And they do this for forty days! It gets harder and harder to whip up that shout of enthusiasm morning after morning when old Goliath is still out there. But there are churches doing this! Working up a shout! I love to be where people are shouting in the Spirit, and I know that if we waited to get the job all done to shout, we would be a very silent majority (or minority, as the case may be). I am not opposed to shouting. But it is one thing to whip up enthusiasm in the sanctuary, and it is another thing to face this gigantic challenge and ask the question "What are we doing about it?" What about this giant that confronts us day by day, year by year, convention after convention? The giant is still out there, and not much is effectively being done. The Israelites were not having any victory at all! They were going through the motions—polishing, marching, shouting. But there he was—still boasting, bluffing, putting them down. They had a hard time keeping their morale up.

They were not only confounded but also they were divided in their assembly. Young David came out to visit his brethren, and he heard the report; he heard the bluff and boast of Goliath. And he began to talk to the men. "What is the king going to do about this? He's going to give his daughter to anyone who kills Goliath, you say? Well, why doesn't somebody do it?!" About that time David's brothers heard what he was saying. His oldest brother, Eliab, was angry with him. "What are you talking about, you young sprout? What are you here for? I know—you left your few skinny sheep in the wilderness to be a sightseer." And then David asked the question, "Isn't there a cause? Isn't there something that ought to cause a person to commit himself even unto death for the honor and glory of God? Isn't there a cause? I don't ask these questions just because I'm a curious sightseer. I ask these questions because a cause is at stake here—a vital, important cause."

But there was the divided army of Saul, criticizing instead of uniting together. How happy the devil must be when he sees God's people quarreling with one another instead of fighting the enemy. It happens all too often that God's people, instead of marching shoulder to shoulder against this common enemy—this common challenge—take it out in berating one another. Jesus said it would be that way just before His second coming—that the servants would be beating their fellow servants and eating and drinking with the drunken instead of being faithful in stewardship. That was the spirit among these brethren of David's. "Here's our upstart young brother, and he might just take this fellow on! What an embarrassment!" So they mocked and belittled him. These are days that challenge God's people not to quarrel or fight with one another, but to join hand in hand and heart to heart to do our utmost to get this job done. Oh, I pray that God will give us such a melting in these days—and it may take persecution to get us melted together—that He can look upon a people not fragmented in so many different directions but willing to join hearts and hands and efforts together to face this foe.

THE GLORIOUS CAUSE

David claims before his brethren that there is a cause big enough to call all to support it. He is saying in other words, "Brethren, why are we divided? Why are we quarreling about this matter. Isn't this cause big enough and serious enough that we all ought to be pulling together instead of pulling apart? Isn't there a cause here that demands the utmost that we have to give?" And I want to say, yes, indeed, there is a cause so magnificent, so monumental, that it must reach out and take hold of us and all of our assets. When Jesus was on trial the scribes, Pharisees, and Sadducees came together unitedly against Him. There was a cause big enough to make these disagreeing, quarreling Pharisees and Sadducees unite together—that was to get rid of Jesus. There was a cause big enough in World War II to make the Russians and the Americans join together against the common foe, Hitler's Nazi Germany—a cause big enough to make disagreeing people fight together on the same side. And I am declaring to you, friend, with deep commitment, there is a cause big enough to make us rise above whatever divisions might hinder us and unite to promote the gospel of the Lord Jesus Christ, to get on with the task of reaching the unreached multitudes. There is something that will lift us above our playing with toys, our jealousies, our paralyzing fears, and our ineffectiveness, something that will demonstrate that the battle is God's.

This cause was a sacrificial cause. Look back in chapter 16, verse 19. "Saul sent messengers unto Jesse, and said, Send me David thy son, which is with the sheep." Jesse had several sons, and the older ones had gone into battle. Saul wanted his youngest, and I believe, the loveliest one of all. Saul asked for him. When the king asks for your son what do you do? You give him your son. It might be hard to see him go; it might be hard to give up from your home circle your youngest, your dearest. But when the king claims him, you must let him go. That is what King Jesus is doing today—He claims our sons and our daughters. I have a desire for the church —a desire that God will speak to some of our young people and lay His hand upon them and say, "I want you in the front lines of this battle." We do need people behind the ranks. We need people back here that will funnel in the ammunition and keep a supply line open. We need that. But we have to have people in the front line of this battle, and I am telling you that we are in a day when the world has conveyed to this generation such a spirit of love for ease and comfort and plenty that fewer and fewer are hearing the call and making the commitment to join the front line ranks in this battle. There is a shocking, startling lack of young people who are rising up in their early years and saying, "God is appointing me a place in the front lines of this battle, and I commit myself to it." How long has it been since your church has been honored by one right out from among your families that has heard and announced God's call into missionary or evangelistic service for Christ? Let us pray as Jesus said—pray the Lord of the harvest that He will send forth laborers into His harvest. We sing the song, and I love it, "Give of thy sons to bear the message glorious, Give of thy wealth to speed them on their way. Pour out thy soul for them in prayer victorious, And all thou spendest Jesus will repay." If we will make the commitment and the sacrifice, He will repay.

Jesse not only gave his son, however. He gave of his means to support that son. The very next verse says that he loaded a donkey with food supplies to send along with him. He would not send his son to be a drain upon the army but to be a contribution to the army. And you can read at a later place where Jesse did it all over again—another food supply was sent to the army as they were going forth. I thank the Lord for what is being done in our churches. I do not have it in my heart to berate anybody over lacks, because much is being accomplished and I thank God for it. But we must do more. Some mission boards are in arrears because of inflation and expansion of missionary work. We are not giving less each year, we are giving more. But we're still not giving enough to keep up with the acceleration of inflation and enlargement of the work.

I have seen some real sacrifice. This is probably one of the greatest values that I saw during our years in Korea —I witnessed a sacrificing people. I am not just talking about Christian people, I am talking about the Koreans in general. You have heard about people lying on beds of spikes. Why do they do that? They do it because of a basic background philosophy that we ought to commit ourselves totally to whatever ideal we assent to mentally, that an ideal of the mind should have the priority over any kind of physical gratification. This is a basic Oriental philosophy that runs through their religions. It comes to its very highest when people are filled with God's Spirit and endued with that kind of basic philosophy. I could relate many stories of people that I have known, and others that I have heard about in Korea, and their almost unbelievable sacrifices. I knew one lady who, when money was needed to make an investment in the church, shaved her head and sold her hair (to a company making wigs for Westerners). She put the money into the missionary offering, and grew another head of hair. She had the spirit of sacrifice! I think of another case that I knew where a widow and her children were surviving on a very little income. She had a very small section of rice paddy and one cow. When an appeal came for support for the cause, she sold the cow, put all the money from it into the offering, and went back to her family with no milk supply. You say that is unreasonable. It does seem unreasonable, the way we look at things. But that's what sacrifice causes people to do— things which in the eyes of ordinary human thinking appear unreasonable. I knew very personally a man who gave his house. He had only one very humble little house. But a demand came for means for the church, and he sold his house, put most of the money into the cause, and moved into a rented place. That is sacrifice to see the battle won. No wonder that Korea is open to the gospel today when there are people with that kind of spirit responding to the call of the gospel of Christ.

I would just like to suggest to us some small sacrifices we can make. One thing we can do is to fast a meal a week and put the equivalent value into our missionary offering. That would be good several ways. It would be good for us to have that spiritual discipline, and to cultivate a more intense spirit of prayer. It would probably be good for us physically to withdraw from eating at least one meal a week. It would be good for the missionaries to have that time spent each week in prayer for them, and it would be good for the treasurer for us to put the meal's equivalent as an extra offering into the missionary fund. You cannot beat that kind of winning! I would suggest something else that we have been doing in our family for a number of years. At Christmas time we total all of our Christmas giving, whether within the family or outside the family, and we match this amount with a special Christmas missionary offering, not a regular offering, but a special missionary offering over and above everything else. You may say you do not have money for that. If so, I question your priorities. If there is any time that we ought to celebrate missions, it is Christmas time. That is what Christmas is all about—God's giving His Son to come down to an unreached, lost planet to reach and win its inhabitants for eternal life. I commend these ideas to you for your serious consideration.

This cause was sacrificial, but it was also a spiritual cause. Look in chapter 16, verses 13 and 14. "The Spirit of the Lord came upon David from that day forward. . . . But the Spirit of the Lord departed from Saul, and an evil spirit from the Lord troubled him." Saul had the mechanics. He had a big army (at the latest count over 200,000 men). He had spears, he had armor, and he had armor bearers. But he did not have the Spirit of God, and without the Spirit of God all of his army was a sorry spectacle out there, shouting for the battle and marching back in fear and defeat day after day. He didn't have the Spirit. On the other hand, there was a shepherd boy who had the Spirit of God upon him, and he won the battle over the host of the Philistines.

David said the battle was God's battle. David could say that—not everybody can. There is a time and a place we can reach when we can all say that our battle is God's battle. When we make the kind of sacrifice David made and the kind of commitment David made to a cause as high and sacred as that cause, then we can truly say it is God's battle and He is going to show His victory. David did not say that before he had made a tremendous commitment. He had committed himself to going out single-handed against the mighty giant Goliath. He was only a little stripling, we are told. I think of a stripling as a young teenager, 17 or 18 years of age, very ruddy of cheek. This young boy went out against Goliath, and Goliath sneered at him. "You come out against me as if I were a dog—I'm going to feed you to the birds." And David said, "The birds are going to have a meal, alright, but it's not David they're going to be eating! It's a Philistine banquet they're going to have! It's because I come out not with sword or with spear. I don't come just with mechanics. I come in the name of the Lord of Hosts, hallelujah!"

It was a successful cause. What a beautiful story! This is the part we all like. David with his five stones—and he only used one—brought down Goliath! A preacher friend of mine was speaking in Bible college chapel one time about Goliath. He said, "Goliath was so surprised! Nothing like that had ever entered his head before!" What a stupendous victory! It was just the kind of victory that God loves to give to His people when they accept the cause! But when they are quarreling among themselves and hanging their heads and running with fright from the monumental task, God doesn't bestow this kind of victory. I really believe that is one of the reasons why we are not seeing any more victories than we are today in the church. There is not enough unity about this cause, not enough commitment back of this cause. There are not enough young people rising and saying, "This cause is so big, this cause is so compelling, that if I never have a nice automobile or a wonderful home, or money in a bank account, I'm going to join the front ranks." Let's pray that God will raise up some who will say, "There is a cause and, like David of old, if I don't have a lot of means at my disposal—if it's only five smooth stones and a sling —with the Spirit of God, I, under God's direction and empowerment, can be an instrument for victory in the hands of God.

O Lord, claim our sons and our daughters. Claim our purses and our persons. Claim all of our assets, and help us to know how to direct them for your glory. Help us to adopt personal goals that will let us, as a part of your great army, move toward victory!

13

BATTLE PLAN FOR VICTORY

Nahash, king of Ammon, had died. As a courtesy David sent messengers of kindness to Hanun the new King. They were fiercely insulted and treated as enemies. Then, because Hanun anticipated that David would retaliate, he initiated war against Israel. The ensuing battle plan affords us some fine points of strategy for victory.

THE COMMITMENT OF OUR RESOURCES

Hanun had bought the help of Syrian and Mesopotamian mercenaries, which alone vastly outnumbered all of David's forces. In addition the Ammonite army came out against them. So Israel faced a two-front battle, the Ammonites before them and the mercenaries behind.

The Church faces at least a two-front battle today as well. We speak of the home and foreign fronts, but we should recognize that it is all one battle. It is easy to misquote the Great Commission and conclude we should go **first** to Jerusalem and Judea (the home front), **then** to the uttermost parts of the earth. But Jesus said "both . . . and," not "first . . . then." He knew this would be a two-front battle, and we cannot wait to start on the second front until we have concluded the home-front engagement. It is so easy to give an undue proportion of emphasis to one front while neglecting the other. Let it be remembered that we are not winning at all unless we are winning on both fronts!

Joab, David's chief of staff, used wise strategy when he sent the best soldiers where the challenge was greatest. He "chose out of all the choice of Israel, and put them in array against the Syrians" (I Chronicles 19:10). If we are wise, we will do no less than that in our spiritual battle today. Half the world is still unevangelized nearly 20 centuries after the Great Commission was given. We send more than 90 percent of our gospel workers to less than ten percent of the needy population of the world. And it is common to insist that the best should stay at home, because they are "needed so much here." Is it right that one group hear the message a 1,000 times while a much larger group still waits to hear it even once?

The apostles of Jesus did not stay at home to build strong churches. They hearkened to the Lord's commission and went out to the nations in need. God helped "lay people" to start and strengthen churches at home and even in distant places.

Here is prime strategy: send the best where the need is the greatest.

THE COOPERATION OF OUR FORCES

Joab led the assault against the mercenaries, while his brother, Abishai, commanded the battle against Ammon. Joab said, "If the Syrians be too strong for me, then thou shalt help me: but if the children of Ammon be too strong for thee, then I will help thee" (I Chr. 19:12). While fighting on opposite fronts these brothers were engaged in a common cause, and they acted like it. There was a necessary division of forces, but it was not a carnal division from envy or strife. These brothers were not fighting for their own personal honor but for the good of their country and the honor of their king. The very next chapter (I Chronicles 20) tells of Joab's follow-up assault upon Ammon and Rabbah, and II Samuel 12:26-30 fills in the details. When the capital city of the enemy was at the point of surrender, Joab sent for King David to come and gain the honors of victory and the crown of the vanquished king as his own. Here was a man who did not battle for his own honor but in honor of his king. If we could duplicate his spirit today and labor strictly for the honor of Christ, it would be easier to gain effective cooperation in missionary endeavor!

A little later Abishai showed a similar spirit. David was almost overcome by the giant Ishbibenob, but Abishai hurried to his rescue and smote the giant. The people declared, "Thou shalt go no more out with us to battle, that thou quench not the light of Israel" (II Sam. 21:17). What a beautiful spirit for fighting men to have! The honor of their king was the prime concern. It must be so in the Church as well!

There just must be closer cooperation of Christian forces if the engagement to evangelize the nations is to be successfully completed. Without eliminating any of the "divisions" in the army, can we not find it possible to submerge some of our own personal interests and coordinate our efforts in honor of our King's command? Let us help one another as Joab exhorted his brother, and let us win a battle against overwhelming odds.

At the U. S. Center for World Missions in California, 64 different mission agencies are cooperating with a primary goal of penetrating new people groups with the gospel and providing a church for every group by the year 2000. These are primarily non-holiness missions. If such cooperation is possible and desirable for them, how much more should we, who profess the highest possible grace, plan and share in a common strategy for victory!

COURAGE FOR THE BATTLE

Joab exhorted, "Be of good courage, and let us behave ourselves valiantly for our people, and for the cities of our God: and let the Lord do that which is good in his sight" (I Chr. 19:13). Numerically the forces were lopsided, but Joab had great confidence that God could give a victory. He had done so before, and He could do it again, if His men would work together for His praise. They were totally committed and courageous in the fight, and God honored them with an overwhelming victory.

It is high time for the church to be totally involved in world missions. It must be a central emphasis in homes, schools, churches and camps. It cannot be a secondary issue when Jesus put it in first place. We cannot afford to go on with each separate group working in total independence while we get farther behind every day in carrying out the Great Commission. The "marching orders" of our King must shape our strategy. His honor is at stake; His purpose must constrain us; His will must swallow up our own as we unite in a total effort for victory. Surely there is a way whereby our separate efforts can be united in an overall strategy that the Lord will bless with success. He routed the Syrians and the Ammonites and gave climactic triumph to His people. He is the same God still. **He is waiting for us to plan and achieve victory in His name!**

14

STRENGTH FOR THE BATTLE

After King David had overcome Saul's murderous threat against his life and had been established as King over all Israel, he desired to build a temple to the Lord. God responded by saying that David had been a man of war, and that his son would be a man of peace who would build the temple. So David went forth to battle in renewed earnestness, determined to put down all opposition from the outside of Israel and prepare the way for a peaceful reign by Solomon.

In each succeeding engagement David gained victory and brought home trophies of wealth to enrich the temple that was to be built. His heart was in that Holy Temple, for it would be God's own dwelling place!

Following that series of conquests, David wrote a Psalm of victory in which he magnifies God's power to deliver us from our enemies. Here is part of it as recorded in II Samuel 22:18-20, 38-40,

> *He delivered me from my strong enemy, and from them that hated me: for they were too strong for me. They prevented [confronted] me in the day of my calamity: but the Lord was my stay. He brought me forth also into a large place: he delivered me, because he delighted in me. . . . I have pursued mine enemies and destroyed them; and turned not again until I had consumed them.*

And I have consumed them, and wounded them, that
they could not arise: yea, they are fallen under my feet.
For thou hast girded me with strength to battle: them
that rose up against me hast thou subdued under me.

THE ENEMIES OF DAVID

Observe first *the enemies of David.* In verse 18 he says they
were strong and hateful. In fact, they were too strong for him.
Perhaps he was thinking back on the days when he was fleeing
from the armies of Saul. Forced away from his own homeland and
later opposed by his own men, David was apparently overwhelmed
with adversity. He was at the total end of his resources. But
"David encouraged himself in the Lord his God" (I Sam. 30:6).
That was the turning point; from there his fortunes began to
ascend steadily.

David described the intensity of opposition that was against
him, saying "the floods of ungodly men made me afraid" (II Sam.
22:5).

The force of opposition was like the mighty sweeping waves
of the sea which totally submerge all that stands in the way. He
further says that he was in distress (v. 7), a word that literally
means to be forced apart or crumbled to pieces. It seemed that
his powers to withstand the pressure had been totally overcome
and that he was being pulverized by the opposition.

I wonder if you have ever felt that way. Have you been in
circumstances when it seemed that trouble came on top of trouble, and you were totally devastated? I have been there, and I
know the depression that can follow such circumstances.

David's enemies included those who were once his friends.
King Saul had witnessed David's victory over Goliath but had
turned into a demon of jealousy, pursuing the good man with murderous hate. David's wives had either turned against him or had
been taken from him.

His enemies also included those who were perpetually the enemies of God's people. Once the Amalekites came upon David's
camp while he and his men were in battle, and took away all their
possessions, including wives and children. When this was discovered, David's own men spoke of stoning him to death. Driven from
his home country with wives and families gone and friends turned
to enemies, what will a man do? Will he be "forced to pieces,"
smashed to bits? We shall soon see.

First, let us name some of those foreign enemies. They included the Philistines, Ammonites, Syrians, Moabites, Zobah and the Edomites. What an array of enemies! David believed that God wanted them to behold Him as victor over all the earth, and it was David's task to bring them under the sway of a righteous rule. So he went on and fought them.

I wonder if you have identified your enemies. Can you name them? Are they habits, people, circumstances, spiritual forces, or a combination of all of these? If you can identify your opposition, you are already on the way to victory!

THE CRY OF DAVID

Observe with me secondly *the cry of David.* In verse 7 he says, "In my distress I called upon the Lord, and cried to my God. . . ." In himself he was going to pieces, but he was not left to himself. "He encouraged himself in the Lord." He had discovered the wonderful secret of God's near presence.

David came to the end of himself and began to reckon on God's help. That is where success begins. Jesus began His Sermon on the Mount by saying, "Blessed are the poor in spirit: for theirs is the kingdom of heaven" (Matt. 5:3). That is a fundamental principle of the kingdom: spiritual victory begins just beyond our own strength. We can never reach it by ourselves. In the world success is to be measured by our human resources. But spiritual success begins just beyond the limit of our abilities. When we see that we are too poor to provide the necessary resources, we are at the threshold of the kingdom!

To whom do you cry in your despair? Does anybody hear? Are you strengthened as you cry, or does your despair multiply? Your crying will lead either to despair or deliverance. Which is it?

David, I remind you, cried to the Lord. He didn't just cry; he cried to Somebody Who could deliver him. Ah, that makes a world of difference. Everybody needs to cry sometimes, for life is too big for all of us at times. But the most helpful crying is unto the Lord. He hears and is interested.

Something happened when David cried. This psalm of victory includes a most graphic portrait of God's intervention. In highly figurative language, the Psalmist has God riding on the wings of the wind and flying with the help of a cherub. Clouds, darkness, thunder and lightning, ocean waves and earthquakes—

these and more joined to celebrate God's coming to deliver one man from trouble!

God, you see, is a real Deliverer. He doesn't just make boasts. He may wait for a time, but then He comes, just in the right instant, and delivers His servant.

My family had gone to Korea strictly by faith without the support of a missionary board. We believed God had called us to a specific task of helping a large group of churches find the way to revival and renewal in the truth of holy living. After several months of delightful labor among 150 churches and as many students in the seminary, there came a day when my wife heard the doctor diagnose her case as cancer. She must return home to the States at once for surgery.

I had prayed almost all the preceding night for the revival I desired but apparently without touching the throne of grace. But with this news of my wife's problem I bowed my head at my little desk and began to pour out my heart to God. "Lord, we came here at your bidding; we are your servants and we are working wholly for your glory. If you want this endeavor to end abruptly in apparent failure, that is Your decision. We will follow Your direction."

Suddenly God was in that small room of a Korean-style house with its dirt-floor kitchen and its rice-paper doors. The glory of Heaven flooded my soul, and God spoke rich assurances to me. "I know where you are," He said, "and I have everything under control. You need not fear to trust me. I will take care of you."

Early the next morning, while hundreds of Korean believers were in a dawn prayer meeting interceding for my wife, that tumor began to shrink away, and it has never come back to this day.

Yes, our God is a mighty Deliverer!

Here is a different kind of deliverance. One of our Korean friends was Pastor Lee Tai Joon. He was pastoring in Chun Ju when the Communists invaded the South and began to dominate the country. When they came to his town they asked Pastor Lee to give them his church for a headquarters. This he refused, since it had been dedicated exclusively to the service of God. So they threw him into prison, where he was kept for weeks while he wondered what would be his fate.

One night after midnight he was taken with several other prisoners in a truck and hauled to the outskirts of the city. Here, watched by guards, they were allowed a smoke break—the guards' courtesy to those about to be slain. Pastor Lee didn't smoke, but he did pray. He "cried unto the Lord." And God heard him. As they were again loading into the truck, there suddenly appeared a man in uniform, dignified and authoritative in his bearing. He carried a document with him which named Pastor Lee as one under orders to be released. The guards were surprised, but they obeyed orders, and Pastor Lee was accompanied away by the officer and led to a place of safety. Then the strange official disappeared and was not seen again.

Pastor Lee was confident it was an angel of God, like the one who delivered Peter from his death cell in Jerusalem so long ago!

Yes, our God is a deliverer. Name your enemy and call upon the Lord. He hears the honest and earnest cry!

THE DELIVERANCE OF DAVID

Next, consider *the deliverance of David.* In Verse 40 he says, "Thou hast girded me with strength to battle." God didn't come and do everything for the man while he himself was wholly passive. David had to fight his best, and God gave strength to win. He wants His people to be good soldiers, and He designs that every conflict will make us better disciplined for spiritual warfare.

It is impossible, of course, for sinners to battle their way to victory over sin, although God often requires some self-discipline in overcoming bad habits and breaking off wrong relationships. God forgives and justifies without human works gaining any merits whatever. Then, when we have enlisted for spiritual warfare, He begins to strengthen us for the battles that we encounter. He expects us to grow and become strong, because our eternal sphere of service is going to involve authority, and we need to develop readiness and faithfulness here in this earthly arena.

One of the reasons why the Lord helped David so quickly and so powerfully was because of his righteous conduct. With only one or two exceptions, David's responses under pressure were "after God's own heart"—very much like those of Christ Himself. The deep consciousness of favor with God—of a pure conscience—gave him great confidence that his cry would be heard. He was realizing the truth expressed by the Apostle John: "Beloved, if our hearts condemn us not, then have we confidence toward God. And whatsoever we ask, we receive of him, because we keep his commandments, and do those things that are pleasing in his sight" (I John 3:21-22). Centuries later another writer said, "He that is pure in heart has the strength of ten."

A person with covered sin cannot have such confidence and strength. The Psalmist said on another occasion, "If I regard iniquity in my heart, the Lord will not hear me" (Psa. 66:18).

Do you have this confidence that God hears when you call upon Him? Is your conscience pure? If not, that is a matter for your urgent attention. Begin to pray honestly about your sin to God, confessing fully and trusting Him to forgive. If you are willing to forsake sin in the fullest possible way, then God is willing to take it away and blot out the record of your past.

It appears that David may have gone too far in appealing to his own righteousness, however. Nine times in verses 21 to 25 of the text chapter he asserted that his victory was according to his own righteousness. "The Lord rewarded me according to my righteousness: according to the cleanness of my hands hath he recompensed me," he began. It is a wonderful thing to have that consciousness of purity before God, and it is good to know that God does reward those who are pure before Him. But it is a subtle danger to begin boasting of our own righteousness and claiming privileges as a consequence.

If our belief is correct that this psalm was written right after victory over all of his foreign enemies, then it was not long afterward that David fell into sin with Bathsheba, the wife of Uriah, the noble soldier in his army. And it illustrates the warning of St. Paul, "Let him that thinketh he standeth take heed lest he fall" (I Cor. 10:12). After such a great string of victories it was apparently easy for the good man to rest in his goodness, and that is a natural prelude to a fall of disastrous proportions. It serves as a warning to all of us that while it is our privilege to enjoy a righteousness that pleases God, our gaze must never rest on that righteousness in ourselves but always on the mercy and merits of Christ.

THE PRAISE OF DAVID

This psalm illustrates finally that all praise is due to God for the deliverance He provides for His people. David exulted in these words:

> *The Lord liveth; and blessed be my rock; and exalted*
> *be the God of the rock of my salvation. It is God that*

*avengeth me, and that bringeth down the people under
me, and that bringeth me forth from mine enemies: thou
also hast lifted me up on high above them that rose up
against me: thou hast delivered me from the violent
man. Therefore I will give thanks unto thee, O Lord,
among the heathen, and I will sing praises unto thy
name (vv. 47-50).*

And this very psalm was part of the fulfillment of that last promise: singing praises unto God's name.

All praise was due unto the Lord, because the battle was just
too big for David. Left to himself he would have failed totally.
But God came to the rescue at just the right moment.

He still does that for those who obey Him and trust His
power. We may remember the story of General Doolittle, who was
involved in the B-25 raid over Tokyo during World War II. His
plane was ditched in the Pacific due to damage sustained in the
raid. For days he floated in a life raft, hoping for rescue. Food
supplies failed, and strength as well. Ultimately he sighted an
island and began to work his raft in that direction. But there was
an undertow that kept pushing him away and thwarting his best
efforts. In desperation he cried unto the Lord, and it seemed that
a mighty hand took that raft and brought it ashore in spite of
the counter current. He was willing to give all praise to God for
the deliverance. At his own utter end, he cried for help and found
it, because God is listening for needy people to cry unto Him.

On a foreign mission field my wife was taken to surgery for
a serious abdominal rupture. I was not there in the hospital
because I had not received word of the emergency until too late
to reach her bedside. The surgeon was unknown to her, and that
caused her some concern. As surgery began he said to his assis-
tant, "This case is hopeless; it is totally impossible to save her
life. Infection has spread until there is no use to proceed with the
surgery." But the assisting doctor knew the family, so she
pleaded, "Doctor, these are praying people; let us do our best and
see if prayer makes any difference." When my wife left the hospital in a much improved condition, that doctor said to her, "Mrs.
Yocum, I want you to know that every day you live you are a
walking miracle. This kind of recovery is not possible to medi-
cine. It has to be a miracle!"

Several factors produced concern the night before surgery as my wife was contemplating her situation. I could not be contacted by phone and knew nothing of the emergency; she did not know the surgeon or his ability as a doctor; she was alone, separated from every member of her family. But there on her bed she opened her Bible to Psalm 50:15, "Call upon me in the day of trouble: I will deliver thee, and thou shalt glorify me." Immediately there came a wondrous rest to her spirit, and she slept easily all night. God did deliver her miraculously, and she has been living to His praise ever since.

Yes, God is interested in the individual. He leads nations to battle and rules over all the earth. But He hears the earnest cry of a single troubled soul and hurries to give help. So if you are one of those troubled people, overcome in the battle, cry unto Him Who is "mighty to save, and strong to deliver."

15

GOOD SOLDIERS OF JESUS CHRIST

W hile Jesus was here on earth He sent His twelve disciples to witness to the people of Israel. When He arrested Saul of Tarsus on the Damascus Road, He informed that zealot that his task was to evangelize the Gentile world. That seemed like a lopsided assignment: 12 men to a small nation and one man to the rest of the world.

But that one man, known later as the Apostle Paul, had a firm determination: to finish the entire task while he lived. He really expected to see the whole world evangelized in his generation, and then Jesus would come.

St. Paul was frustrated in his task. Hindrances, including some five years spent in prison, arose to prevent his continuing as he desired in reaching the end of the earth. But he was not discouraged or ashamed of his mission. He committed to young Timothy the task of continuing with the ministry of the Gospel.

Here are his words of challenge, as found in II Timothy 2:1-4,

Thou therefore, my son, be strong in the grace that is in Christ Jesus. And the things that thou hast heard of me among many witnesses, the same commit thou to faithful men, who shall be able to teach others also. Thou therefore endure hardness, as a good soldier of Jesus Christ. No man that warreth entangleth himself with the affairs of this life; that he may please him who hath chosen him to be a soldier.

THE SOLDIER'S PREPARATION

Notice that this charge begins with a "therefore." St. Paul used that word frequently, stringing his logical thoughts together with it. If we follow the string backward to its beginning in Chapter 1, we find the credentials of Timothy which prepared him to be a soldier.

First, there was his good heritage. Both his mother and grandmother had imparted knowledge of the Scriptures to him, which grounded him in faith and salvation (v. 5). Anybody who has such a rich heritage is placed under obligation to share its benefits with others. God does not allow His children to be enriched simply to enjoy the riches alone. We are stewards of the gifts which God has bestowed upon us, and we shall surely be called into account for the use we make of them and the returns which the Lord shall receive from the investment He has made in us. The parable of the talents (Matthew 25:14-30) with numerous other passages surely establishes this fact beyond question.

Timothy had, moreover, *a gift from God.* We are not told just what it was. Perhaps Alexander Maclaren was correct when he said that gift included the whole commitment of divine resources that fitted Timothy for his work and which were given from the Holy Spirit. Every believer, like Timothy, has some spiritual gift from the Spirit which prepares him for a suitable ministry. It will not be exactly the same as Timothy's, and it will not involve the same type of ministry in every case. But each believer must use his gift for the cause of Christ or be found speechless before Christ's examination, like the one-talent man of Matthew 25.

Finally, Timothy had the *spirit of power, of love* and *of a sound mind.* He was not given the spirit of fear, the Apostle said. Naturally, Timothy was a weak sort of person who had physical ailments and probably a rather timid disposition. But he must not be fearful, Paul urged, because he had the Spirit of God in his life and had faith in the powerful Word of God.

Surely the Lord expects to develop the same qualities in all of His soldiers: power, love and a sound mind (self-discipline). We are not to be controlled by native tendencies of timidity, fear, and self-preservation. God's Spirit bestows power, love and self-discipline.

Do you realize that the early church never used the "Great Commission" as the challenge to move believers out in witnessing? The Holy Spirit working in their lives did just what St. Paul said. God's power was expressed through their lives of love for others, which brought all their resources under a disciplined purpose to spread the gospel. We must have the same motivation today!

THE SOLDIER'S STRATEGY

We have seen the credentials of Timothy; *now let us observe the strategy* which the Apostle purposed for Timothy to employ. *He was to commit what he had learned to faithful men, who could teach others also.* Isn't that simple? But it worked in the early church, and it will work today. Each person who has received the saving truth of Christ is to teach it to somebody else, who in turn can teach it to others. By this process Paul believed the gospel could go to the end of the earth before the end of the age.

That simple strategy was in the mind of Jesus when He spoke His Great Commission. It was a teaching commission. Kenneth Wuest, in his expanded translation of the New Testament, puts the Great Commission in these words, which are true to the original language:

> *Having gone on your way therefore, teach all the nations, making them your pupils, baptizing them into the Name of the Father and of the Son and of the Holy Spirit, teaching them to be attending to carefully, holding firmly to, and observing all, whatever things I enjoined upon you (Matt. 28:19-20).*

The one main verb of that commission is *"teach."* The things which were enjoined on you, Jesus said, must be so faithfully taught to others that they will attend carefully to them, hold them firmly, and observe them all faithfully.

My friend, this is the pressing challenge of the whole church today. It must begin in the home, as it did with Timothy. He was taught so faithfully by a mother and grandmother that he was made wise unto salvation himself and was prepared to bear the message to others. But today there is entirely too much shifting of this responsibility. Children are turned over to Dr. Seuss books, TV programs, and baby sitters, until they grow up with very little understanding of God's Word, the Christian faith, or of a personal responsibility to be stewards of Christ.

The same strategy is found in the closing chapter of the Bible, Revelation 22:17, "And the Spirit and the bride say, Come. And let him that heareth say, Come. And let him that is athirst come. And whosoever will, let him take the water of life freely." At the heart of that beautiful appeal is this challenge: "let him that heareth say, Come." If you have heard the gospel invitation you must invite somebody else to come. Those who haven't heard must be invited by somebody who has heard. Then, having heard, they must tell somebody else. By this means everyone who is athirst will soon have a personal invitation to take freely of the water of life!

Oh, let us not fail concerning this simple New Testament strategy!

Soldiers are needed today as they were in that ancient day so that the strategy can be victoriously implemented.

THE SOLDIER'S DISENTANGLEMENT

In the passage quoted earlier in the chapter the soldier's qualifications are suggested. There must first be a *disentanglement* from the affairs of this life. The soldier lives in a physical, social, and financial world, but he must be free from entanglements therein, so he can serve effectively for his country. Surely it is so for Christian soldiers! They are to be in the world but not of the world (John 17:15-16). They are to "use the things of this world, as if not engrossed in them" (I Cor. 7:31, NIV). They are to function within the cultural milieu of this world without being pressed into its mold. That requires constant and careful watchfulness!

When I enlisted in the Army Air Force during World War II, I learned something about disentanglement. This was during depression days, and I had just finished my college education so was without financial resources of any kind. Pay for a cadet was only $45.00 per month. Even so I was required to make a will, so that in case of my death all my earthly possessions would be given to the right beneficiary. I was expendable!

Soldiers—G.I.s, as they were called—soon learned that they were to live without a lot of special privileges that civilians enjoyed. Haircuts were not according to a soldier's fancy but by a standard "G.I. cut." Hair was short-cropped all over, with no variations! G.I.s were not asked what cut or color of suits they desired. They were issued olive drabs. (Along with many others, I loathe the color to this day.)

The menu was not ordered to suit the individual taste. If a man didn't like the meal he could go without, but that would not change the menu for tomorrow. The standard reply to any complaint was this: "You're in the Army now!"

Today there is a "prosperity gospel" being widely proclaimed, but it does not come from the Scriptures. It is designed by people who are already entangled in this world to justify their overinvolvement. The cross of Jesus is not a mark of prosperity in this world but of scorn and rejection by the world.

St. Paul wept over those "whose end is destruction . . . who mind earthly things" (Phil. 3:19). They are "enemies of the cross of Christ," he said with tears. What shall we say of those who intend to be fully involved in the prosperity of this world, seeking what makes them feel good, going after earthly pleasures, and following earthly fashions wherever they lead? Are they not also enemies of the cross, in danger of destruction at the end of their way?

God wants all believers to be soldiers. He does not divide His people into two sections, soldiers and softies. In fact, the softies have no part in the kingdom of God. I Corinthians 6:9-10 declares that the effeminate (that is just what "softy" means), along with adulterers and homosexuals, shall have no entrance into that eternal kingdom.

Every believer is meant to have a ministry of some kind. It was never God's intention that the church should be divided into "ministry and laiety;" that distinction came from Roman Catholicism, and it has done irreparable harm to the ministry of the Church. I Corinthians 12:4-7 explains that every believer has a gift, a ministry, and a work to do: "Now there are diversities of gifts . . . there are differences of administrations . . . and there are diversities of operations . . . but the manifestation of the Spirit is given to every man to profit withal." The word "administration" is the same which in other places is translated "ministry." Every believer is to have some ministry. Oh, when will this truth be grasped by the whole Church and implemented with a soldier spirit?

In wartime, everybody is expected to be involved. There is gasoline rationing, conscription of forces, defense plant employment, and shortage of many luxuries. Every family must be willing to give a son or daughter. Likewise, the church is on a battleground, not a playing field, and everybody must be involved. If we are just playing at the job we are losing the battle. It is a time that demands real soldiers! The forces that are arrayed against the Church of God are formidable and determined. The battle lines are being drawn tighter and tighter. There is no middle ground between involvement and betrayal! Nobody can be merely a casual "believer," sitting comfortably on the sidelines and hoping to share the rewards of victory. God is calling for soldiers who are totally committed to service and victory in Jesus' name. It is time for a large body of comfortable, compromising professors of religion to make a real decision: to get into the battle on the side of a cross-bearing, Christ-honoring band of true soldiers or abandon the pretense of genuine Christianity altogether. (The former choice is infinitely preferable, of course.) Nothing less than this can follow from application of such scriptures as Matthew 16:24-25, "If any man will come after me, let him deny himself, and take up his cross, and follow me. For whosoever will save his life shall lose it: and whosoever will lose his life for my sake shall find it."

THE SOLDIER'S DISCIPLINE

The good soldier must manifest, secondly, a *disciplined endurance of hardness.* The words "of a sound mind," in II Timothy 1:7, really mean "self-disciplined." And self-discipline, in the ultimate sense, means the commitment of every resource to the fulfilment of a worthy goal in life. Surely the supreme goal should be the fulfilment of God's will and the promotion of His glory. Any personal goal in conflict with this should be abandoned at once as unworthy of any commitment.

In the military service of our country, soldiers are put through boot camp, field maneuvers, obstacle courses and training exercises in order to develop a disciplined readiness for the real battle. God does no less than this in preparing His soldiers for conflict. They are allowed to experience opposition, to carry heavy loads, and to engage in minor conflicts with enemy forces so they can develop toughness and endurance.

Ours is an age of softness right now, however. Rev. J. Kessler of Taylor University recently compared the young people of today with those of the 1970's. In that former decade, he said,

American young people had a striking idealism, believing that by getting involved they could change society and the world. They joined the "Jesus People movement," the Hippie communes, and numerous street demonstrations to get involved.

In the 1980's, Kessler continued, young people are different. Many have concluded that they individually can't make any real difference in the world. Consequently, they have turned in upon themselves with selfishness born of despair. The self-esteem movement is a natural by-product of this turn-about, with people now primarily interested in themselves and what they can gain to enrich their experience of the moment.

Into this milieu there still comes the call of Jesus Christ for volunteers who will forsake all else to serve in His Army. They must embrace a cause high above themselves and their personal pleasure. They must be willing to be as a grain of wheat dropped into the earth and covered up, ready to die in order to bring forth much fruit. They must be ready to forsake home and family, houses and lands, and even their own life, to enlist in a crusade for truth and holiness, and supremely for the honor of their Captain, Jesus Christ.

The rewards will not be immediate cash in the bank or a higher popularity rating. They are not promised constant fun and excitement. There will be deep valleys filled with enemy forces, long trails paralleled by enemy emplacements, and desperate struggles to overcome. But ultimate victory is assured, and the final rewards are out of this world! Eternity will be filled with praise for the triumph of Christ and for the privilege of serving in the ranks of His faithful ones.

Robert Sharpe was an American soldier in the Korean Conflict. At 18 years of age he was thrown into the thick of battle. His outfit was overrun by Communist forces, and many were left beaten and dying on the ground. In the night Sharpe recovered from coma and found himself severely wounded among his dead and dying buddies. Some of them he buried; others he endeavored to help by tearing some of his own clothing into bandages for their wounds. Then, having done all he could to help them, he started a long effort to get back to American Forces. Hiding by day and wandering through forests and fields by night, he foraged on seeds and herbs. Sick and weak, he finally staggered into an American camp and was hurried to the hospital. But Sharpe didn't beg to go home to his family. Over and over he said, "Let me go back, let me go back." His heart was in the battle for freedom and with his fallen buddies.

That is beautiful dedication and triumphant self-discipline! Can we not see the same for the cause of Christ? May we not behold a band of healthy, well-trained young people, who rise above mere pleasure-seeking and pour out their very lives to save others and to carry out the mandate of their Lord? Please grant it, O Christ!

THE SOLDIER'S DEVOTION

The good soldier is finally *devoted to His Master.* "No man that warreth entangleth himself with the affairs of this life," said the Apostle, "that he may please him who hath chosen him to be a soldier" (II Tim. 2:4). That we may please our Lord and Leader: that is our high motivation for self-sacrificing service. When the battle is over and the victory is won, we will all report to the Master and answer for our opportunities and accomplishments. We will not be saved because of service but because of mercy and grace. The rewards that are handed out, however, are for faithful service rendered.

In November, 1945, I was on the Battleship West Virginia, moving slowly toward the coastline of the United States. For many months I had been part of the military effort to free the Pacific area from Japanese occupation. V. J. Day had come and gone, and by a prearranged formula the Air Force was releasing men from active duty. My turn had come, and I was among hundreds of servicemen who were on their way home.

Early one morning almost every man was on deck pressing toward the bow of the ship, straining his vision to catch the first sight of our homeland. We had been informed that today we would dock at San Pedro, California. Suddenly somebody called, "There it is!" Peering through the early morning mist, one after another saw the dim outline of faraway mountains against the sky. Home was in sight! I had left my dearest friend—the fiance of my twin sister—in a humble grave on Guam. Others on this ship had also faced the cost of war. Some had been wounded. They had all been separated from family and friends. The Army made no apologies. This was war and it was costly. But now victory had come, and we were going home in triumph.

Finally the harbor was reached. Our feet stood on friendly shores, and I soon made a train trip halfway across the continent to a glad reunion with relatives.

Today I have on my wall a certificate which says, "This is to certify that Lt. Col. Dale M. Yocum, having served faithfully and honorably, was retired from the United States Air Force on the 19th day of October, 1979." It was signed by the Chief of Staff of the United States. That certificate on the wall really doesn't amount to very much, though I am glad to have it. But there is another award I seek after: the words of my beloved Master when He shall say, "Well done, thou good and faithful servant; enter into the joys of the Lord!"

Oh, I want some sheaves to lay at His feet in that day! No appeal of dollars, or titles, or earthly acclamations shall be allowed to dim the hopes of that celebration. To see Him face to face, Who gave His all for me, and to give back something to Him that will please Him forever—that is high motivation for me now.

While writing this [March 1987] I am fighting a battle against cancer. The doctors give no hopes beyond two years at best, and six months at the least. Eternity seems very real today. My God is able to heal, and it is my expectation that He may deliver me for His glory. But whether He does or not is of no great concern. My supreme desire is not to live long on the earth but to please Him Who has chosen me to be a soldier. If He is pleased to take me home before Christmas that will be glory for me—to be forever in His presence! If He chooses to leave me longer on earth, it will be to pour out all my life for His praise. He alone is worthy. He has chosen me, and I am His soldier!

Are you a soldier? Have you enlisted to support the greatest cause in the universe? Have you bowed at the feet of Jesus and pledged your life to Him without reserve? Every hardness will be rewarded abundantly, and life will have supreme meaning—in His high and holy service!

16

HOME-TRAINED SOLDIERS

In the story of the first human battle, there is one aspect that deserves further amplification. It is recorded in Genesis 14:14, "And when Abram heard that his brother was taken captive, he armed his trained servants, born in his own house, three hundred and eighteen, and pursued them unto Dan." The climactic victory has already been recounted, a magnificent tribute to home training.

A major thesis of this book is that Bible battles illustrate principles of missions for the Church. So by analogy this lesson teaches us the importance of preparing home-trained missionaries. To put the matter briefly, *every Christian home should be a missionary training center!*

THE NEW TESTAMENT PRECEDENT

Observe first *the New Testament precedent* for such training. In the days of the early church, there were no Bible colleges, missionary boards, printing presses, magazines, books, airplanes or computers. Yet they reached the known world in their generation. They had the authority of the Great Commission, and they took its directive most seriously.

The primary command of that commission is to teach others. Paraphrasing, it says, "As you go, teach others, and teach them to teach still others." And before the Day of Pentecost was past, the ministry of teaching had begun. After 3,000 were converted, "they continued steadfastly in the apostles' doctrine." Doctrine means teaching. A teaching program began in which the believers were grounded in the Christian faith and were prepared to teach the faith to others. St. Paul summarized the method in his instructions to young Timothy: "The things that thou hast heard of me among many witnesses, the same commit thou to faithful men, who shall be able to teach others also" (II Tim. 2:2).

St. Paul illustrated the method in his ministry at Ephesus. After he left the synagogue he "separated the disciples [those being taught], disputing daily in the school of one Tyrannus. And this continued by the space of two years; so that all they which dwelt in Asia heard the word of the Lord Jesus, both Jews and Greeks" (Acts 19:9-10). Paul did not evangelize Asia alone. He continued in the school, training disciples. And they went forth to make more disciples. By this method the world they knew was covered with Gospel light.

Central in the method was the role of the Christian home. For over 200 years there were no church buildings as we know them today. The church centered in the home. In fact, there was in Ephesus a church in the house of Aquila and Priscilla before St. Paul began his ministry in Tyrannus' school. He had left them in Ephesus at the time of his first visit (Acts 18:18-21). Before his return they had taught Apollos and sent him forth as a mighty proclaimer of Christ the Messiah. Doubtless they contributed much to the strength of the Ephesian church. Wherever they went—to Rome, to Corinth, and then to Ephesus—they had a church in their house. And they followed the New Testament pattern of teaching.

House churches were family centered. In Philippi, for example, Paul and Silas went into the house of the jailor, directing the entire household to faith in Jesus as Savior. "And they spake unto him the word of the Lord, and to all that were in the house. And he took them the same hour of the night, and washed their stripes; and was baptized, he and all his, straightway" (Acts 16:32-33).

According to two late manuscripts, Acts 16:27 identifies the Philippian jailor with Stephanas of I Corinthians 16:15, "Ye know the house of Stephanas, that it is the firstfruits of Achaia, and that they have addicted themselves to the ministry of the saints." Isn't that a beautiful description of a Christian family, working as a unit for the extension of the gospel of Christ!? Whether this is the same person as the jailor or not, the passage does highlight the family-centered nature of the church in its ministry.

Although mothers had their responsibility for guiding and guarding the household, the father was to take the lead and assume responsibility. Ephesians 6:4 places that responsibility clearly: "And, ye fathers, provoke not your children to wrath: but bring them up in the nurture and admonition of the Lord."

There are a multitude of professedly Christian homes today where fathers are shirking their duty as educators in the home. One poll has found that in church homes the father spends less that three minutes per day, on the average, in talking about God. They may excuse themselves by saying that Sunday Schools and Christian Day Schools now take care of the training responsibility. That excuse will not stand, however, when we realize that 80% of a child's fears, values and attitudes are fixed by age six. Moreover, beyond age six, and until adolescence, children are generally hero worshipers, and the father is usually the hero—especially if he does have some heroic qualities.

Fathers may further argue that they just do not have time to spend in giving Christian training to their children. This also is a flimsy excuse for such dereliction of duty. In I Timothy 5:8 the Apostle declared, "If any provide not for his own, and specially for those of his own house, he hath denied the faith, and is worse than an infidel." To "provide" means to look ahead and make adequate arrangements. The passage includes material provisions, but it also covers plans for spiritual training. And the father who places his major emphasis on the material and neglects the spiritual training in his family is denying the faith in practice, whatever he claims in his verbal testimony! To be sure, there are many fathers today who are overworked and struggling to keep up with a difficult economic situation. However, it is right at this point that the teaching of Jesus applies with real force: "Seek ye first the kingdom of God, and his righteousness; and all these things shall be added unto you" (Matt. 6:33).

Thrilling news has recently come out of Communist China. Whereas there were some 1,000,000 committed Christians there when the country went under Communism, now there are conservatively estimated to be from 30 to 50 million Christians! They demonstrate what can happen when public Christian assemblies are closed and training is centered in the home.

Those Chinese fathers have not found it easy to train their children in the Christian faith. But they know that if they don't do it, nobody else will. So, though pressed into hard labor in a Communist state, and though persecuted for their faith, they have done the job in noble style.

In the light of such an example, how can Christian parents in our land of rich advantage excuse themselves if they fail?

Another excuse advanced for neglect of home training for missionaries is that the child may not be called of God to do missionary work. Again the excuse falls flat. The Great Commission was given to the entire church, not just to the apostles. It is the one supreme imperative which Jesus gave His Church to be completed before His return to earth. This *must be done*, He insisted (Mark 13:10). How can a person—child or adult—participate in the life of the church at all if not in the supreme task of the church? And how can they participate in that task if they do not have training in what the task is, and how they can share in its achievement? True, not every child will be called to be a foreign missionary. Nevertheless, the child will grow to be more effective in any other role in the church if well instructed in the Church's major purpose.

The lack of effective missionaries today is a crisis of serious proportions. Part of the reason is surely that children in Christian homes are trained for material involvement and money-making rather than for participating in the supreme task of the church. Any believer will be better prepared to be a banker, lawyer, teacher or farmer for the glory of Christ, if it is understood that every occupation of Christians must in some way contribute to the accomplishment of Christ's commission. And surely many more would hear God's call to full-time service if they were trained concerning the seriousness of the task.

It would be just as reasonable to say, "I will not train my child to be a farmer (or a moneymaker by any other means) because I don't know God is calling them to that work" as to say, "I will not train them for missionary work because God may not call them to that ministry." It is certain that He has some purpose for them that will contribute to the advancement of the church toward its goal. And that goal includes living for the spread of the gospel to all the world. Jesus said, in Mark 8:35, "Whosoever will save his life shall lose it; but whosoever shall lose his life for my sake and the gospel's, the same shall save it." There are only two options available, you see: to save one's life or to lose it. To save it one must lose it for Christ *and the gospel.* We are not free to live for Christ and to omit all responsibility for His gospel. To live for Him truly is to live for His gospel as well. And that means to be involved in extending the gospel where it has not been heard.

The conclusion is obvious: *if we are to train our children to follow Christ, we must also train them to share His gospel with others who have not received it.* And that means missionary training! How much farther the church would be advanced toward its goal if every Christian home had followed this rule!

THE NEW TESTAMENT PRINCIPLES

Having considered the New Testament precedent, may we observe further the *New Testament Principles.* They are beautifully illustrated in the practice of Aquila and Priscilla, as set forth in Romans 16:35, "Greet Priscilla and Aquila my helpers in Christ Jesus: who have for my life laid down their own necks: unto whom not only I give thanks, but also all the churches of the Gentiles. Likewise greet the church that is in their house."

The home of these noble Christians was a school of the Word. In Acts 18:26 we read of them, "When Aquila and Priscilla had heard [Apollos], they took him unto them, and expounded unto him the way of God more perfectly." St. Paul had stayed in their home as he taught. Now they were teaching others. Tent makers had become the teachers of a real scholar, because they had a superior grasp of the Scriptures.

Here is an absolute imperative for our children: *they must learn the Holy Scriptures.* If they are to grow in Christ they must know the Word of God. I Peter 2:2 says, "As newborn babes, desire the sincere milk of the Word, that ye may grow thereby." It should not be at all surprising that young people brought up without consistent training in the Word, including memorization of the same, are stunted and remain spiritual pygmies!

If our youth are to be of high morals and live consistently holy lives, they must have the Word stored in their hearts. Psalms 119:9 makes it plain: "Wherewithal shall a young man cleanse his way? by taking heed thereto according to thy word." If they do not have a good grasp of the Word, they will be inclined to weakness before temptation.

If the faith of our children is weak, it may well be because they know so little of the Word. St. Paul said to young Timothy,

"From a child thou has known the holy scriptures, which are able to make thee wise unto salvation through faith which is in Christ Jesus" (II Tim. 3:15). Faith comes by hearing the Word of God, we are told (Rom. 10:17), and that is true of children as well as adults.

If the Scriptures make people wise unto salvation, then it is most vital that your young people know how to use the Scriptures to bring others to salvation. Conviction and conversion must be based on the Word as it is applied by the Spirit. Timothy was a good illustration of this fact.

Today, however, there is an appalling lack of knowledge of the Word. It is alarming when propagandists for false doctrines have a better grasp of the Scriptures they use (or misuse) than our people have to present the truth of full salvation!

A recent Gallup poll revealed that only one-half of the people who attend church can name the four gospels, less than half know who preached the Sermon on the Mount, and less than half could name even three of the Ten Commandments! Of evangelicals, only three out of ten read the Bible daily.

With statistics like these it is no wonder that disciplined, committed missionary candidates are in short supply! Our Christian homes must become schools of the Word of God.

The home of Aquila and Priscilla was further a place of sacrifice for missions. In Romans 16:4 St. Paul says that this couple "have for my life laid down their own necks: unto whom not only I give thanks, but also all the churches of the Gentiles." Though it was life-threatening to do so, here was a home and family totally committed to supporting and promoting the gospel.

Such sacrificial commitment was common in New Testament days. Jesus commissioned all of His followers to be witnesses, and the original word for witness was *martus*, from which our word "martyr" comes. Originally the word simply meant one who bears witness. It was the early church that added the dimension now included in the word: to die for a cause. Now we must use two separate words to keep the meaning distinct.

Historically it has been commonplace for adults, and even young children, to lay down their lives rather than to deny Jesus Christ as their Savior. It was my privilege to minister in Ethiopia when the Communist regime was imposing tight control over the people. I witnessed young children six to twelve years of age being herded at gunpoint into an indoctrination center for a brainwashing ritual. But upon inquiry of pastors and parents, I learned of not a single child who had denied the faith. Some of them were so brave that they challenged their own parents to greater boldness for Jesus' sake.

It is hard to maintain a spirit of sacrifice in a land of abundance where people tend to be preoccupied with the "cares and riches and pleasures of this life, and bring no fruit to perfection" (Luke 8:14).

This writer will always be grateful that it was his privilege to grow up during depression years, when every nickel was highly valued, and never was a crust of bread left uneaten on the plate because it was too much work to chew it! Disciplined self-denial on the farm during those days has served me well in mission lands where the food served by gracious hostesses has included fresh sea slugs, octopus tentacles, and bread baked on cow-manure discs.

The need is most urgent for pastors and parents who exemplify and teach the spirit of sacrifice.

Aquila and Priscilla made their home a place of constant emphasis on missions. Whenever a missionary came their way, whether Paul, Apollos or another, their home was opened to receive and entertain the missionary. What a rich legacy for children in the home!

Again my mind is enriched with memories of times like that when I was brought face-to-face with missionaries from Japan, India, or other faraway places. The sight of great snake skins and sun helmets and the stories of pagan people transformed by divine grace were powerful influences toward Christian service. When missionary personalities were not present, there were missionary biographies which had almost as strong an influence in shaping character and commitment.

With so many wonderful books and magazines available now concerning missionary life, there is really no good reason why children in Christian homes cannot become personally identified and involved with the missionary cause.

From his childhood David Livingstone had a map of Africa on his wall. Going to Africa was becoming his lifelong goal before he went there in person.

Christian parents who allow their children's walls to be plastered with pictures of burly football stars, rock musicians or TV personalities should not be surprised if those children lack spiritual sensitivity or desire to bear the cross of Christ. What they are permitted to gaze upon and dream about will gradually mold their desires and characters.

Missionary maps can be placed on bedroom walls, with pictures of families serving abroad, and children can be taught to pray regularly for those families.

As often as children spend money for candy or other trivia, they can be trained to put an equal amount of money into a missionary bank. This can be put directly into a missionary offering, or it can be saved to finance a personal visit to a mission field at a proper age.

Letters written to missionary children provide excellent experience in English usage as well as identification with people on a field of service.

These are just a few of the ways in which creative parents can keep the challenge of missions before their children. The rewards can be infinitely greater than the investment.

Finally, Aquila and his wife got personally involved in missionary efforts. On at least three occasions they moved to a new city and opened their home for missionary pioneering. Supported by their trade of tent making, they gave themselves to the advancement of the gospel.

Not every family can move to a foreign field. But some could move to a new city and help to plant a church, giving valuable support to a pioneering pastor.

There are many ways our families can get fully involved in outreach for Jesus' sake. I have just concluded an intensely exciting missionary convention, where people have been trained to get involved for missions. One young boy had gathered more than 40,000 aluminum cans and sold them for $200 to put into the offering.

No wonder there was excitement! And no wonder there were 14 young people who came forward to confess that God was speaking to them about possible Christian service, and they were willing volunteers!

The noble family of Aquila did not bear arms in bloody combat. But they did enter a much more noble warfare. Some day we will be able to behold all the trophies of battle which they present to their glorious Captain! Along with them may there be a multitude of other households present, in which parents have trained their children to be Christian soldiers!

17

WAR WITH
THE LAMB

The Lamb of God is the central figure in the whole Bible, and certainly the central figure in The Revelation. He is mentioned 28 times as the Lamb in this one book, and He is always in the midst of the activity. He is central both in earth and heaven. It is He Who ties them together and makes a bridge between. There is no way from earth to heaven except by Him.

Revelation 17:12-14 describes a decisive battle in which the Lamb, Jesus Christ, gains a sensational victory over the beast, the antichrist.

> And the ten horns which thou sawest are ten kings, which have received no kingdom as yet; but receive power as kings one hour with the beast. These have one mind, and shall give their power and strength unto the beast. These shall make war with the Lamb, and the Lamb shall overcome them: for He is Lord of lords, and King of kings: and they that are with him are called, and chosen, and faithful.

THE ENEMIES OF THE LAMB

Observe first the character of those who are against the Lamb. They are kings without a kingdom: "kings which have received no kingdom as yet." What does that mean? It means they are title lovers—men who want honor and dignity of high office, whether they have lasting authority or not.

Once I was invited into the living room of a leader to wait for his arrival at home. While there alone I saw that on each of the four walls of the room was a large diploma announcing that he was the recipient of a doctor's degree. On one wall there were two, making five altogether. I knew that one degree had been conferred as an honor for some of his achievements. Curious about the others and knowing he'd never traveled to those countries for graduate study, I took names and addresses from them and made some investigation. To my surprise I found there were no such institutions as described in the diplomas. At some of the addresses there was nothing but a common dwelling house. Upon inquiry I found that the man had arranged for a conferral ceremony for himself, and with much fanfare received the honor of bestowal of the degrees. A large picture had been made of him with all of them before him at his desk, and it was prominently displayed in the institution of which he was a part.

Kings without a kingdom are like that: empty titles; honor without responsibility.

But these kings in Revelation were given authority for one hour with the beast. They are the one-hour people, who for one hour of playing king give all their rights and strength in service to the beast—for good or ill, forever.

What a contrast! Jesus gives to His faithful followers the privilege of reigning with Him forever and ever, and the masses refuse Him. The beast let men play king for one hour, and they sign away all their liberties to follow him!

This is not abstract theorizing; the armies are now being prepared. Some are surrendering to Christ, enduring the moral and spiritual warfare that is involved and investing all their hopes in Him today. Others are passing Him by and following the call of "king for an hour," led on by the spirit of antichrist.

Several years ago there was a rock concert at Hampton Beach, New Hampshire. The youth went wild and tore up the town in one hour. A Christian worker spoke to one of the young men, asking "Are you happy?"

"I'm miserable," was the quick response; "all I've been doing is experimenting. None of these kids is happy. Sex is just an escape. They're looking for anything that satisfies, even *for one* hour. Nothing is real. There seems to be no future, so we just stop and get off for a few days."

There are plenty of places for the one-hour people to stop and get off these days: rock festivals, drug busts, easy sex, pornography, liquor, sadism by VCR, and many more. They never mind the consequences; they think just of the hour of sensation. Nothing seems real beyond that. So the antichrist is enlisting his forces for the showdown with the Lamb.

Those against the Lamb are of one mind also. They think alike. They have succumbed to the powerful mind-makers and given up their freedom of thought for a mindless conformity.

One of the most powerful influences to bring such mental conformity to pass is modern television. It is largely controlled by people who make this present world appear more real and attractive than the world to come. It makes fantasy more appealing than truth, and that is basic to brainwashing.

Malcolm Muggeridge, a former media man himself, wrote in *Christ and the Media* concerning the people who control the content of television:

> [Their views are] predictable on matters like abortion, the population explosion, family planning, anything whatever to do with contemporary *mores*, as well as aesthetics, politics, and economics, . . .
>
> This, in my experience, applies as much to the religious broadcasting department as any other; if not more so. . . . Consensus-making and promoting, I should say, is to be seen historically as an instinctive preparation for some sort of conformist-collectivist society which lies ahead whatever may happen, all that is in doubt being the precise ideology which will characterize it (pp. 51, 52).

Television, in short, works powerfully to bring its viewers to the same beliefs as those who control the content of the programs. It brings them to a one-mind position.

Dr. George K. Pratt, writing in *Modern Home Medical Advisor*, attempted to describe the drift from mental health to mental illness. There is no sharp break between the two, but a kind of continuum along which a person moves toward insanity. Describing the midpoint of the line, Dr. Pratt said, "an individual may come to be thought of by his neighbors as 'queer' in some way.

Perhaps he shows a fanatical streak about religion or politics .
.." (p. 835).

The important thing to note here is that the neighbor's opinion is the indicator of a halfway point to mental illness. If the
person does not think as the neighbors do about religion, or is
viewed as "queer," then by definition he is half-crazy.

But Jesus made it perfectly plain that His followers would
be thought strange by the world. In fact, He said they would be
hated by the world around them, and that a sharp sword of separation would cut them apart from popular acceptance in the
world's society.

With such a definition of mental illness, or the point halfway
to it, and with the increasing power of the state to handle those
viewed as mentally incompetent, one can visualize the powerful
urge to think just like everybody else does. The antichrist will
utilize this urge to conform the populace to his own patterns and
designs.

Notice in Revelation 17:17 that God does not stop this powerful influence from working: He rather encourages it! "For God
hath put in their hearts to fulfil his will, and to agree, and to give
their kingdoms unto the beast, until the words of God shall be
fulfilled."

This is one of the most serious truths in all the Bible! There
comes a point where truth rejecters are rejected by God, and
instead of drawing them toward Himself He sends them error and
lets it control them.

St. Paul described the process in II Thessalonians 2:10-12.
Speaking of the antichrist, who comes with full satanic power,
Paul described his working:

> . . . with all deceivableness of unrighteousness in them
> that perish; because they received not the love of the
> truth, that they might be saved. And for this cause God
> shall send them strong delusion, that they should believe
> a lie: that they all might be damned who believed not
> the truth, but had pleasure in unrighteousness.

Many times in the Bible the solemn fact is reinforced: if people do not grasp God's saving truth when they recognize it as
TRUTH, then the truth will be taken from them and they will
be turned over to the spirit of error, which will be embodied fully
in the antichrist when he comes. How very important it is then

to receive the love of the truth and be saved while the truth shines clearly! To reject truth is to ask for error and deception, and it will surely come!

Ultimately there is no middle ground between saving truth and damning error, between Christ and Antichrist.

THE LAMB

Notice second *the character of the Lamb Himself.* The word "Lamb" clearly identifies Him with the earth. That is where lambs are always born. The fact that in Heaven He is still the Lamb "as it had been slain," shows that He will never release His human form, or cease from His personal identification with needy earthlings.

In Isaiah 53:5 and 7 it is revealed that the Lamb is the Messiah and our Savior:

> *He was wounded for our transgressions, he was bruised for our iniquities: the chastisement of our peace was upon him; and with his stripes we are healed. . . . He is brought as a lamb to the slaughter, and as a sheep before her shearers is dumb, so he openeth not his mouth.*

He is the world's only sufficient and necessary sin bearer. He is God's sacrifice for the sin of all of us, even for me.

This Lamb was poor. The word is commonly used for a pet lamb, one whose mother is gone and who will perish unless taken in and cared for. He had no place to lay His head but found resting places among the trees. He was so poor that He was born in a borrowed stable and laid in a borrowed manger. He sailed across the Sea of Galilee in a borrowed boat and fed the multitudes with borrowed bread and fishes. Finally, He was crucified on a borrowed cross and buried in a borrowed tomb.

But today He is not living on borrowed things. All of heaven and earth belong to Him, and He is Lord of all! Why did He become so poor? So He could make us rich. "For ye know the grace of our Lord Jesus Christ, that, though he was rich, yet for your sakes he became poor, that ye through his poverty might be rich" (II Cor. 8:9). Do not despise His poverty; it was for your sake. Rather seek in Him the true riches that will never fade away!

This Lamb was pure. "Ye were not redeemed with corruptible things . . . but with the precious blood of Christ, as of a lamb without blemish and without spot" (I Pet. 1:18-19). The Old Testament sacrifices had to be without physical blemish, and God's Lamb was without moral or spiritual blemish. Neither friends nor foes, angels nor devils, found any sin or inconsistency in Him. He was finally crucified because He claimed to be what He actually was, God's Messiah.

If we do not love Him today, it is because there are serious spots in our moral nature. But He came to remove those spots and to make us like Himself, a church for Himself, "not having spot, or wrinkle, or any such thing; but that it should be holy and without blemish" (Eph. 5:27). So we may seek Him for His cleansing.

God's Lamb was persecuted. The mob was moved against Him and screamed for His blood. The weakling, Pilate, pressured by the throng, submitted Jesus to their passions and let Him be treated more meanly than any other man. Isaiah foresaw it and declared, "Many were astonished at thee; his visage was so marred more than any man, and his form more than the sons of men" (Isa. 52:14).

It is so easy to be swept away by the mob. Peer pressure is as strong today as it was there in the street of Jerusalem. And multitudes are letting their characters be formed under pressure from the crowd rather than under the sovereign hand of God.

I joined a bunch of boys one time in mocking a little orphan girl coming onto the school ground. Poorly dressed in one of her father's overall jackets, hair disheveled, face and hands chapped and cracked from a severe winter's cold, and overworked by having to be mother and housekeeper as well as grade school student, she should have been an object of everybody's pity. But I joined the taunting crowd and laughed as Ruby burst into tears and ran into the one-roomed schoolhouse to escape our cruelty.

My sister learned what happened, and so did my parents. The next day I had to go back and apologize to that dear orphan girl for my thoughtless mistreatment. And there are some reading these lines who ought to go right to Jesus and apologize because they have joined the crowd and rejected Him, after all of His loving condescension and suffering for their sins. Will you do that today?

God's Lamb was patient. While He suffered "He opened not His mouth." He did not scream back at those who screamed at Him. Never did He give blow for blow, or curse for curse. In the garden He met those who came for His arrest and stopped them short by His calmness. To Judas the traitor He spoke, "Friend, wherefore art thou come?" He was still a friend to His fallen follower. And He is still your friend, and mine, regardless of how far we may have wandered away, and how deep we have fallen into sin and failure.

To the noisy rabble that came for Him He said, "This is your hour, and the power of darkness." Yes, they were the one-hour people, swept along by passion, unmindful of the long-range consequences of their action. Jesus was in their hands, and they could have their way with Him for that hour.

My dear friend, Jesus is in your hands today also. It is your hour of decision. This is your hour to decide—for Him or against Him. This is your hour; but remember, eternity belongs to Him. And He will have the last word. It will be a word of eternal judgment.

Although the Lamb bears an earthly identification, He wins a mighty kingly victory! "The Lamb shall overcome them," exclaimed the angel who spoke with John. This is surely one of the most sensational events of all time or eternity.

Look at how unbalanced the battle is! A great beast against a little lamb! Chapter 13 of The Revelation shows the power and influence of the beast. "All the world wondered after the beast. . . . And they worshiped the beast, saying, Who is like unto the beast? Who is able to make war with him?" (v. 3-4). Yes, all the one-hour, one-mind people, who are pressured by the crowd and who fear to stand against public opinion—they follow the beast and worship him.

Do not think he will come with horns and a long pitchfork in his hands. No, indeed! He will have more charisma and magnetism than an Abraham Lincoln, Dwight Eisenhower, and John Kennedy combined. He is pictured as a beast with seven heads and ten horns. He is like a lion, a bear and a leopard all in one. But this does not mean that He is hideous; it means he is strong! He sways the people with his craftiness. He works miracles, controls finances, marches armies, makes dramatic speeches, and moves with all the subtle deception of Satan himself. The common theme of the day is, "Nobody can withstand him!"

But the Lamb overcomes him. It is such a momentous upset that the story cannot all be contained in a short paragraph. Chapter 6 of the Revelation tells of events when the sixth seal is opened and the forces of nature are loosed on the ungodly. Stars fall; the heavens depart like a scroll rolled up; islands and mountains disappear. Then the great men of all kinds—kings and captains, industrialists and philosophers—cry for the rocks to fall on them and hide them from the face of "him that sitteth on the throne, and from the wrath of the Lamb: for the great day of his wrath is come; and who shall be able to stand?" (vs. 16-17).

The wrath of the Lamb! How incongruous that seems. I have seen lots of lambs, but never an angry one. Lambs are playful creatures. They can leap straight into the air with all four feet and come down dancing for joy. They love to play, but never seem angry.

But here the Lamb is angry. He looses the powers of heaven and hurls them at His enemies. Why? Why is the patient Lamb now angry? Because the one hour is past, and eternity is at hand. Because men have callously spurned His mercy, His self-sacrificing love, His costly identification with us in our need. Because men with good minds have forfeited their right of intelligent choice and deliberately followed error instead of truth. They have loved pleasure and despised righteousness. Having spurned mercy and love, they have earned justice and wrath.

Another phase of the victory story, and a climactic one, is given in Chapter 19. It is the story of Armageddon, which was described in an earlier chapter. The outcome is as certain as God's inerrant Word, as sure as God Himself.

Since the resurrection of Christ the final victory has been absolutely assured. The resurrection, Peter said, proved that eternal life in Christ could not be confined in death; He had to rise again! (Acts 2:24).

Yes, the Lamb overcomes the beast and all his allies. He brings an end to Satan's power, to the false prophet, and to all the outworkings of evil in the world. He is King of kings and Lord of lords! He shall reign forever. Do not ever forget it. He seemed small in His earthly beginnings, and to many He still seems very small today. But this is man's little hour, and Jesus is much in the background. Soon He will step forth and assert His might. He will demonstrate that truth must prevail over error, righteousness over sin, and eternity over time. If you are not in His Church today, this is your hour to decide.

THE ALLIES OF THE LAMB

Finally, three words in our scripture passage depict *the character of those who are with the Lamb.*

They are called. Here is the marvel of God's love and mercy: He CALLED us. To all who are sinful, defeated, burdened and bound the Savior says, "Come unto me, all ye that labor and are heavy laden, and I will give you rest" (Matt. 11:28). To church people in danger of being engulfed with the appeal of easy but false religion, He calls, "Come out of her, my people, that ye be not partakers of her sins, and that ye receive not of her plagues" (Rev. 18:4). You see, He keeps calling to us, drawing us to Himself, encouraging us to follow Him and to overcome to the end.

His calls are not noisy and boisterous. He does not compete with the rabble to get our attention. The Prophet spoke of Him and said, "He shall not cry, nor lift up, nor cause his voice to be heard in the street" (Isa. 42:4). He may call through a hymn, through a sermon, through a personal testimony, through some gracious providence, or directly through the Word. The Spirit of God speaks softly to the heart, and you must listen in order to hear Him. You can make enough noise to still His voice. He is still calling, but you can fail to hear Him.

There is power in His call to save you. When Jesus stood at the tomb of Lazarus and called, "Lazarus, come forth," there was power in the command to bring him back to life and out of the tomb. His Word has the same potential today when spoken in the power of the Spirit. When the Word calls to you and says, "Repent ye therefore, and be converted, that your sins may be blotted out, when the times of refreshing shall come from the presence of the Lord" (Acts 3:19), if you listen you can repent and you can be converted, and you will receive the refreshing of the Lord in your spirit!

Yes, He is tenderly calling today. So listen, and hear, and live!

His followers are CHOSEN. This does not mean that God arbitrarily selects some to be saved and others to be lost, without regard to their personal responses. The key to His choice is seen in Ephesians 1:4, "[God] hath chosen us in [Christ] before the foundation of the world, that we should be holy and without blame before him in love." It is not that we are chosen to be in Christ, although that is also true. It is rather that those who are in Christ are chosen to be holy and blameless. God has chosen a way whereby all can be in Christ if they will. The final invitation of the Bible is this: "Whosoever will, let him take of the water of life freely" (Rev. 22:17). Many other passages assert that whosoever will believe on Christ may be saved.

The choice is ours, therefore, whether we will be in Christ or not. In fact every person is choosing between Christ and Antichrist. Whether we are on the side of the Lamb or against Him is our choice, and we are choosing in this our hour of decision. What is your choice? Remember, this choice is for all eternity. Those who choose Christ will be victors forever. Those who choose the popular way with the one-hour people will suffer shame and defeat without end. But after the battle is over it is too late to choose sides. The choice is now!

In the Roman catacombs are grave markers of many people who died in the persecutions of that city. One Christian left these words: "Victorious in peace and in Christ." One without Christ had this epitaph: "Live for the present hour, since we are sure of nothing else."

We Christians are perfectly sure of something beyond this present hour, so we choose and we live for eternity which has already begun in our hearts. It is my prayer that somebody reading these lines may make the same choice today.

The followers of the Lamb are also FAITHFUL. They do not live by the impulses of the moment but by an unshakeable conviction of eternal truth. Like Moses, the faithful today are enduring all manner of troubles for Jesus' sake, "as seeing him who is invisible" (Heb. 11:27). Jesus is their prime example and they look unto Him, "who for the joy that was set before him endured the cross, despising the shame, and is set down at the right hand of the throne of God" (Heb. 12:12).

Jesus described those who, because of peer pressure, go along with the multitude and compromise holy principle even in the realm of religion. Hear His words about the last days: "Because of the increase of wickedness, the love of most will grow cold, but he who stands firm to the end will be saved" (Matt. 24:12-13 NIV). Listen to those words again: "the love of most will grow cold!" Those who once had a white-hot love will gradually lose it and settle down into a comfortable conformity. And the strong inference is that they will not be saved at last. It is the ones who stand firm, who endure the cold, and who resist the majority's patterns of conduct who will overcome and be saved.

Believers may expect an increased measure of seduction and opposition as the end approaches. The Bible warns of this very thing. While describing the perils of the last days, St. Paul warns, "But evil men and seducers shall wax worse and worse, deceiving, and being deceived. But continue thou in the things which thou hast learned and hast been assured of . . ." (II Tim. 3:13-14). That is good information for us today.

At the climax of the Battle of Armageddon, John "saw heaven opened, and behold a white horse; and he that sat upon him was called Faithful and True, and in righteousness he doth judge and make war. . . . And the armies which were in heaven followed him upon white horses, clothed in fine linen, white and clean" (Rev. 19:11, 14).

The faithful Christ has waited a long time to fill the earth with His righteousness. He has never resorted to deceitful devices or immoral shortcuts to gain His ends. He has waited for wickedness finally to come to its end and fall under its own weight, as ultimately it must! The prophet foretold it when he said "He shall not fail nor be discouraged, till he have set judgment in the earth: and the isles shall wait for his law" (Isa. 42:4).

His followers are willing to wait also. They believe in His ultimate victory, and they believe it is abundantly worthwhile to follow Him through present delays and apparent reversals, because He is absolutely sure to win in the end.

Soon He shall have put down every opposing force, and He shall sit on the throne of eternal glory and victory. Gathered around Him will be those who were faithful to the end. They will shout the praises of His faithfulness, and He will reward them for theirs. While the followers of the antichrist bewail their short-sightedness and folly, the Lamb's followers will reign with Him forever, rejoicing that they did not allow themselves to be swept along with the one-hour people but that they chose the values that last forever.